ONE MIX
A HUNDRED
CAKES

ONE MIX
A HUNDRED
CAKES

Christine France

This edition published by Parragon Books Ltd in 2013
LOVE FOOD is an imprint of Parragon Books Ltd

Parragon Books Ltd
Chartist House
15–17 Trim Street
Bath BA1 1HA, UK
www.parragon.com/lovefood

ISBN 978-1-4723-3016-1

Printed in China

Written by Christine France
Cover design by Geoff Borin
Photography by Clive Streeter
Home economy by Angela Drake

Notes for the Reader
This book uses both metric and imperial measurements. Follow the same units of measurement
throughout; do not mix metric and imperial. All spoon measurements are level: teaspoons are
assumed to be 5 ml, and tablespoons are assumed to be 15 ml. Unless otherwise stated, milk is
assumed to be full fat, eggs and individual vegetables are medium, and pepper is freshly ground
black pepper.

Garnishes, decorations and serving suggestions are all optional and not necessarily included in the
recipe ingredients or method. The times given are an approximate guide only. Preparation times
differ according to the techniques used by different people and the cooking times may also vary
from those given. Optional ingredients, variations or serving suggestions have not been included in
the time calculations.

Recipes using raw or very lightly cooked eggs should be avoided by infants, the elderly, pregnant
women, convalescents and anyone suffering from an illness. Pregnant and breastfeeding women are
advised to avoid eating peanuts and peanut products. Sufferers from nut allergies should be aware
that some of the ready-made ingredients used in the recipes in this book may contain nuts. Always
check the packaging before use.

Contents

Introduction

Even if you're not a domestic god or goddess, the good news is that home-baked cakes don't have to be difficult or time-consuming. This book is packed with quick-mix cakes for all occasions, so you'll never be short of ideas for easy, irresistible home-baked treats. The beauty of this book is that every single recipe is based on the Basic Cake Mix (see page 10). To make life easier for you, we have done the hard work so that each recipe is complete and you won't need to refer back to the basic recipe every time.

Equipment

The equipment needed for these cakes is found in most kitchens: mixing bowl, sieve, weighing scales, measuring spoons and jug, a wire rack and cake tins.

Good-quality cake tins conduct heat evenly and efficiently for perfect results and will last for years. Basic cake tin shapes include deep round and square, sandwich, ring, Bundt, loaf, spring release and rectangular, and bun or muffin trays. Since cake tin sizes vary between manufacturers, many of the recipes in this book provide the tin's capacity. To find a tin's capacity, simply use a measuring jug to pour water into the tin and note how much liquid it takes to fill the tin.

Mixing bowls in tempered glass or plastic are tough and versatile for mixing. Choose measuring jugs and spoons marked clearly in standard measures.

A hand-held electric mixer does much of the hard work but you can mix by hand with a wooden spoon if you prefer.

Basic Ingredients

The basic cake mix includes plain flour, baking powder, butter/oil/cream/yogurt, sugar/honey/syrup, eggs, vanilla or other flavouring extract, and milk or fruit juice.

Plain flour is used with baking powder, and these must be sifted together to ensure even distribution of the raising agent throughout the mixture. Ratios do vary slightly so always check the quantities in the ingredients list before you start.

Butter gives the best flavour, but it can be replaced by margarine if you prefer. Spreads are usually lower in fat and may give unreliable results. Use softened butter, either at room temperature and beaten until soft, or softened in a microwave for a few seconds but not melted. Oil is useful when a moist texture is required, such as for gingerbreads, and light-flavoured oil, such as sunflower, is a good choice. Cream and yogurt are lower in fat than butter, so these produce cakes with a denser texture and a shorter life.

Either white or golden caster sugar give a light, fine-textured cake, but natural light or dark muscovado sugar can also be substituted to add an extra richness of flavour. Always ensure there are no hard lumps in the sugar before adding to the mix as these may not dissolve. Golden syrup or honey can be used as a substitute for sugar in cakes where a softer texture is required. Demerara sugar is good for sprinkling over the top to add a crunchy topping. Icing sugar is invaluable for fillings and icings, or for dusting over cakes as instant decoration.

Eggs should be medium, ideally at room temperature. If you store eggs in the refrigerator, remove them about 30 minutes before use to allow them to come up to room temperature.

Vanilla extract is the most versatile flavouring to enhance cakes and bakes. For true flavour, make sure to choose bottles marked 'extract' rather than 'flavouring'. Other useful extracts used in this book are almond, coffee, orange flower water, rose water and peppermint.

Milk or fruit juice is added to lighten the mix, and you can choose whole, semi-skimmed or skimmed milk, or fruit juices like apple, orange or lemon. Some recipes may omit this, depending on the balance of added ingredients.

Extra Ingredients

Wholemeal flour, oats or polenta may be substituted for some or all of the white flour or added to the mix to vary the texture and flavour, the amount depending on the balance of other ingredients. Generally, the higher the fibre and coarser the grain, the denser the resulting texture will be.

The simplest way to vary the flavour of cakes is to add spices – cinnamon, mixed spice, allspice, nutmeg, ginger or star anise all work well in cakes. Sift the spices with the flour and baking powder to ensure they're evenly combined with the mix. Finely grated citrus rind will add a light, fresh flavour to many cakes and frostings.

Chocolate cakes are always a favourite and this may be added in the form of cocoa powder, chocolate chips or melted chocolate. It may be necessary to reduce the flour quantity when adding cocoa to some cakes, so make sure to check the recipe.

Fresh or dried fruits transform a simple sponge into a rich special-occasion cake or luxurious gateau. Dried fruits have a concentrated flavour and sweetness and they're great storecupboard standbys. Canned fruit should be drained well, as the extra liquid may upset the balance of ingredients.

Nuts (such as almonds, hazelnuts, walnuts or pecans) or seeds (such as sunflower, pumpkin, poppy or sesame) not only give a crunchy texture to cakes but also add valuable nutrients and fibre for healthier treats.

Top Tips for Successful Cakes

- Turn on the oven before you start in order to preheat it to the correct temperature whilst you're mixing.

- Brush cake tins with melted butter or oil and line with non-stick baking paper to prevent sticking.

- Measure ingredients accurately and level measuring spoons flat with the back of a knife.

- Avoid over-mixing because this can cause a heavy texture – beat the mix until just smooth.

- Bake the cake immediately once mixed because the baking powder begins to act as soon as it's combined with liquid.

- Avoid opening the oven door too often during baking – this reduces the oven temperature and can cause cakes to sink.

- Test cakes carefully for doneness – they should be well risen and golden brown and starting to shrink from the sides of the tin. Sponge cakes should feel springy to the touch.

- To prevent damage, allow cakes to stand in the tin to firm up for a few minutes before turning out onto a wire rack to finish cooling.

Basic Cake Mix

Makes 2 x 20-cm/8-inch sponge sandwich cakes

* oil or melted butter, for greasing
* 175 g/6 oz plain white flour
* 1 tbsp baking powder
* 175 g/6 oz unsalted butter, softened (recipes may substitute oil, cream or yogurt)
* 175 g/6 oz caster sugar (recipes may substitute golden caster, light or dark muscovado sugars, or honey/syrup)
* 3 eggs, beaten
* 1 tsp vanilla extract (recipes may substitute other flavouring extracts, e.g. almond, coffee, orange flower water)
* 2 tbsp milk or fruit juice

This is the basic recipe that all 100 variations of cakes in the book are based on.

For each recipe the basic mix is highlighted ( ) for easy reference, so all you have to do is follow the easy steps each time and you'll never run out of ideas for creative cakes.

Please note that the basic ingredients may vary from time to time so please check these carefully.

Favourites

Chocolate Sandwich Cake

1. Preheat the oven to 180°C/350°F/Gas Mark 4. Grease two 20-cm/8-inch sandwich cake tins and line the bases with baking paper.

2. Sift the flour, cocoa and baking powder into a large bowl and add the butter, caster sugar, eggs and vanilla extract. Beat well until the mixture is smooth, then stir in the milk.

3. Divide the mixture between the prepared tins and smooth the surfaces with a palette knife. Bake in the preheated oven for 25–30 minutes, or until well risen and firm to the touch. Leave to cool in the tins for 2–3 minutes, then turn out and finish cooling on a wire rack.

4. When the cakes have cooled completely, sandwich together with the chocolate spread, then dust with icing sugar and serve.

Serves 8

- oil or melted butter, for greasing
- 150 g/5½ oz plain white flour
- 2 tbsp cocoa powder
- 1 tbsp baking powder
- 175 g/6 oz unsalted butter, softened
- 175 g/6 oz golden caster sugar
- 3 eggs, beaten
- 1 tsp vanilla extract
- 2 tbsp milk
- 140 g/5 oz chocolate spread
- icing sugar, for dusting

Coffee & Walnut Ring

1. Preheat the oven to 160°C/325°F/Gas Mark 3. Grease a 1.5-litre/2¾-pint ring cake tin, preferably non-stick.

2. Sift the flour and baking powder into a large bowl and add the butter, sugar, eggs and coffee extract. Beat well until the mixture is smooth, then stir in the chopped walnuts.

3. Spoon the mixture into the prepared tin and smooth the surface with a palette knife. Bake in the preheated oven for 40–45 minutes, or until risen, firm and golden brown.

4. Leave to cool in the tin for 10 minutes, then turn out carefully onto a wire rack. Whilst the cake is still warm, spoon over half the maple syrup. Leave to cool completely. To serve, top with walnut halves and drizzle over the remaining maple syrup.

Serves 10

- oil or melted butter, for greasing
- 175 g/6 oz plain white flour
- 1 tbsp baking powder
- 175 g/6 oz unsalted butter, softened
- 175 g/6 oz light muscovado sugar
- 3 eggs, beaten
- 1 tsp coffee extract
- 70 g/2½ oz walnuts, chopped, plus extra walnut halves to decorate
- 4 tbsp maple syrup

3

Sticky Ginger Loaf

1. Preheat the oven to 180°C/350°F/Gas Mark 4. Grease and line a 1.2-litre/2-pint loaf tin.

2. Sift the flour, baking powder and ground ginger into a large bowl. Add the oil, sugar, golden syrup and eggs, then beat well to a smooth batter. Stir in the chopped ginger.

3. Pour the mixture into the prepared tin. Bake in the preheated oven for 1–1¼ hours, until well risen and firm.

4. Leave to cool in the tin for 10 minutes, then turn out and finish cooling on a wire rack. To serve, brush the top of the cake with the ginger syrup, decorate with sliced ginger and cut into slices.

Serves 8–10

* oil or melted butter, for greasing
* 175 g/6 oz plain white flour
* 1 tbsp baking powder
  1 tbsp ground ginger
* 175 ml/6 fl oz sunflower oil
  85 g/3 oz dark muscovado sugar
  85 g/3 oz golden syrup
* 3 eggs, beaten
  3 pieces stem ginger in syrup, drained and finely chopped, plus 2 tbsp syrup from the jar
  sliced stem ginger, to decorate

4

Chocolate Fudge Cake

1. Preheat the oven to 180°C/350°F/Gas Mark 4. Grease and line a 23-cm/9-inch round cake tin.

2. Place the chocolate and milk in a small pan and heat gently until melted, without boiling. Remove from the heat.

3. Sift the flour and baking powder into a large bowl and add the butter, muscovado sugar, eggs and vanilla extract. Beat well until smooth, then stir in the melted chocolate mixture, mixing evenly.

4. Spoon the mixture into the prepared tin and smooth the top level. Bake in the preheated oven for 50–60 minutes, until firm to the touch and just beginning to shrink away from the sides of the tin.

5. Leave to cool in the tin for 10 minutes, then turn out and finish cooling on a wire rack. When cold, carefully slice the cake horizontally into two layers.

6. For the frosting, melt the chocolate with the butter in a small pan over a low heat. Remove from the heat and stir in the icing sugar, vanilla extract and milk, then beat well until smooth.

7. Sandwich the cake layers together with half the frosting, then spread the remainder on top of the cake, swirling with a palette knife. Sprinkle with chocolate curls or grated chocolate.

Serves 8

* oil or melted butter, for greasing
* 55 g/2 oz plain chocolate
* 2 tbsp milk
* 175 g/6 oz plain white flour
* 1 tbsp baking powder
* 175 g/6 oz unsalted butter, softened
* 175 g/6 oz dark muscovado sugar
* 3 eggs, beaten
* 1 tsp vanilla extract
* chocolate curls or grated chocolate, to decorate

Frosting
100 g/3½ oz plain chocolate
55 g/2 oz unsalted butter, softened
175 g/6 oz icing sugar
1 tsp vanilla extract
1 tbsp milk

Marbled Chocolate & Vanilla Ring

1. Preheat the oven to 160°C/325°F/Gas Mark 3. Grease a 1.5-litre/2¾-pint ring cake tin, preferably non-stick.

2. Sift the flour and baking powder into a large bowl and add the butter, caster sugar and eggs. Beat well until the mixture is smooth. Transfer half the mixture to a separate bowl.

3. Mix the cocoa powder with the milk and stir into one bowl of mixture. Add the vanilla extract to the other bowl and mix evenly. Spoon alternate tablespoons of the two mixtures into the prepared tin and swirl lightly with a palette knife for a marbled effect.

4. Bake in the preheated oven for 40–50 minutes, or until risen, firm and golden brown. Leave to cool in the tin for 10 minutes, then turn out and finish cooling on a wire rack. Dust with icing sugar before serving.

Serves 12

- oil or melted butter, for greasing
- 175 g/6 oz plain white flour
- 1 tbsp baking powder
- 175 g/6 oz unsalted butter, softened
- 175 g/6 oz caster sugar
- 3 eggs, beaten
- 2 tbsp cocoa powder
- 2 tbsp milk
- 1 tsp vanilla extract
- icing sugar, for dusting

Banana Cake with Caramel Frosting

1. Preheat the oven to 160°C/325°F/Gas Mark 3. Grease and line a 20-cm/8-inch square cake tin.

2. Sift the flour and baking powder into a large bowl and add the butter, soured cream, sugar, eggs and vanilla extract. Beat well until the mixture is smooth. Stir in the bananas.

3. Spoon the mixture into the prepared tin and smooth the surface with a palette knife. Bake in the preheated oven for about 1 hour, until risen, firm and golden brown.

4. Leave to cool in the tin for 10 minutes, then turn out and finish cooling on a wire rack.

5. For the frosting, place the butter and muscovado sugar in a pan and simmer gently, stirring, for about 2 minutes. Remove from the heat and beat in the soured cream and icing sugar. Leave to cool for 30–40 minutes, or until thick enough to hold its shape.

6. Spread the frosting over the top of the cake, swirling with a knife.

Serves 12

- oil or melted butter, for greasing
- 175 g/6 oz plain white flour
- 1 tbsp baking powder
- 85 g/3 oz unsalted butter, softened
- 85 g/3 oz soured cream
- 175 g/6 oz light muscovado sugar
- 3 eggs, beaten
- 1 tsp vanilla extract
- 2 ripe bananas, mashed

Frosting
- 40 g/1½ oz unsalted butter
- 40 g/1½ oz light muscovado sugar
- 2 tbsp soured cream
- 85 g/3 oz icing sugar

Sponge Roll

1. Preheat the oven to 180°C/350°F/Gas Mark 4. Grease and line a 23 x 33-cm/9 x 13-inch Swiss roll tin with the paper 1 cm/½ inch above the rim. Lay a sheet of baking paper on the work surface and sprinkle with caster sugar.

2. Sift the flour and baking powder into a large bowl and add the butter, sugar, eggs and vanilla extract. Beat well until the mixture is smooth, then beat in the milk.

3. Spoon the mixture into the prepared tin and smooth into the corners with a palette knife. Bake in the preheated oven for 15–20 minutes, or until risen, firm and golden brown.

4. When cooked, turn the sponge out onto the sugared baking paper and spread with the jam. Roll up the sponge firmly from one short side to enclose the jam, keeping the paper around the outside to hold it in place.

5. Lift onto a wire rack to cool, removing the paper when firm. Sprinkle with caster sugar, cut into slices and serve.

Serves 8

* oil or melted butter, for greasing
  150 g/5½ oz plain white flour
  1½ tsp baking powder
* 175 g/6 oz unsalted butter, softened
* 175 g/6 oz caster sugar, plus extra for sprinkling
* 3 eggs, beaten
* 1 tsp vanilla extract
* 2 tbsp milk
  115 g/4 oz raspberry jam, warmed

Date & Spice Loaf

1. Preheat the oven to 160°C/325°F/Gas Mark 3. Grease and line a 1.3-litre/2¼-pint loaf tin.

2. Sift the flours, baking powder and mixed spice into a large bowl, adding any bran left in the sieve. Add the butter, sugar, eggs and vanilla extract. Beat well until the mixture is smooth, then stir in half the dates.

3. Spoon the mixture into the prepared tin and scatter over the remaining dates. Bake in the preheated oven for 40–50 minutes, or until risen, firm and golden brown.

4. Leave to cool in the tin for 10 minutes, then turn out and finish cooling on a wire rack.

Serves 8–10

- oil or melted butter, for greasing
- 85 g/3 oz plain white flour
- 100 g/3½ oz plain wholemeal flour
- 1 tbsp baking powder
- 1 tsp ground mixed spice
- 175 g/6 oz unsalted butter, softened
- 175 g/6 oz golden caster sugar
- 3 eggs, beaten
- 1 tsp vanilla extract
- 175 g/6 oz stoned dates, roughly chopped

Fig & Lemon Bars

1. Preheat the oven to 160°C/325°F/Gas Mark 3. Grease and line a 20 x 30-cm/8 x 12-inch rectangular cake tin.

2. Place the figs, lemon juice, demerara sugar and water in a pan and bring to the boil. Reduce the heat, cover and simmer gently, stirring occasionally, for 5 minutes, or until the liquid is absorbed. Remove from the heat and beat lightly to make a coarse purée.

3. Sift the flour, baking powder and cinnamon into a large bowl and add the butter, muscovado sugar and eggs. Beat well until the mixture is smooth. Stir in the lemon rind.

4. Spoon the mixture into the prepared tin and smooth the surface with a palette knife. Spoon over the fig purée and swirl it into the cake mixture with a knife. Bake in the preheated oven for 40–50 minutes, or until risen, firm and golden brown.

5. Leave to cool in the tin for 20 minutes, then turn out and finish cooling on a wire rack. Cut into bars when cold.

Serves 8–10

- oil or melted butter, for greasing
- 200 g/7 oz ready-to-eat dried figs, chopped
- 2 tbsp lemon juice
- 1 tbsp demerara sugar
- 100 ml/4 fl oz water
- 175 g/6 oz plain white flour
- 2 tsp baking powder
- 1 tsp ground cinnamon
- 175 g/6 oz unsalted butter, softened
- 175 g/6 oz light muscovado sugar
- 3 eggs, beaten
- finely grated rind of 1 lemon

Country Fruit Cake

1. Preheat the oven to 160°C/325°F/Gas Mark 3. Grease and line a 20-cm/8-inch round deep cake tin.

2. Sift the flours, baking powder and nutmeg into a large bowl, adding any bran left in the sieve. Add the butter, muscovado sugar, eggs and vanilla extract. Beat well until the mixture is smooth, then stir in the milk and mixed dried fruit.

3. Spoon the mixture into the prepared tin and smooth level with a palette knife. Sprinkle the demerara sugar evenly over the surface. Bake in the preheated oven for 1 hour 20 minutes–1 hour 30 minutes, or until risen, firm and golden brown.

4. Leave to cool in the tin for about 20 minutes, then turn out and finish cooling on a wire rack.

Serves 10

- oil or melted butter, for greasing
- 175 g/6 oz plain white flour
- 70 g/2½ oz plain wholemeal flour
- 2 tsp baking powder
- ½ tsp ground nutmeg
- 175 g/6 oz unsalted butter, softened
- 175 g/6 oz light muscovado sugar
- 3 eggs, beaten
- 1 tsp vanilla extract
- 1 tbsp milk
- 200 g/7 oz mixed dried fruit
- 1 tbsp demerara sugar

Vanilla Victoria Sponge Cake

1. Preheat the oven to 180°C/350°F/Gas Mark 4. Grease two 20-cm/8-inch sandwich cake tins and line the bases with baking paper.

2. Sift the flour and baking powder into a large bowl and add the butter, caster sugar, eggs and vanilla extract. Beat well until the mixture is smooth, then stir in the milk.

3. Divide the mixture between the prepared tins and smooth the surfaces with a palette knife. Bake in the preheated oven for 25–30 minutes, or until risen, firm and golden brown. Leave to cool in the tins for 2–3 minutes, then turn out and finish cooling on a wire rack.

4. For the filling, beat together the butter, icing sugar and vanilla extract until smooth. Spread this mixture on top of one of the cakes and spread the bottom of the other cake with the jam, then sandwich the two together to enclose the filling, pressing down lightly.

5. Sprinkle with icing sugar before serving.

Serves 6–8

- oil or melted butter, for greasing
- 175 g/6 oz plain white flour
- 1 tbsp baking powder
- 175 g/6 oz unsalted butter, softened
- 175 g/6 oz golden caster sugar
- 3 eggs, beaten
- 1 tsp vanilla extract
- 2 tbsp milk

Filling

55 g/2 oz unsalted butter, softened

115 g/4 oz icing sugar, plus extra for dusting

½ tsp vanilla extract

3 tbsp strawberry jam

Carrot Cake with Orange Frosting

1. Preheat the oven to 160°C/325°F/Gas Mark 3. Grease and line a 23-cm/9-inch round deep cake tin.

2. Sift the flour, baking powder, cinnamon and ginger into a bowl and add the butter, muscovado sugar and eggs. Beat well until smooth, then stir in the orange juice, carrots and chopped pecan nuts.

3. Spoon the mixture into the prepared tin and spread the top level. Bake in the preheated oven for 1 hour–1 hour 10 minutes, or until risen, firm and golden brown.

4. Leave to cool in the tin for 10 minutes, then turn out onto a wire rack to finish cooling.

5. For the frosting, place all the ingredients in a bowl and beat until smooth and thick, adding more orange juice if necessary. Spread over the top of the cake and decorate with pecan halves.

Serves 10

* oil or melted butter, for greasing
* 175 g/6 oz plain white flour
* 1 tbsp baking powder
* 1 tsp ground cinnamon
* ½ tsp ground ginger
* 175 g/6 oz unsalted butter, softened
* 175 g/6 oz light muscovado sugar
* 3 eggs, beaten
* 2 tbsp orange juice
* 200 g/7 oz carrots, coarsely grated
* 55 g/2 oz pecan nuts, chopped, plus extra pecan halves to decorate

Frosting
55 g/2 oz full-fat soft cheese

250 g/9 oz icing sugar

finely grated rind of 1 orange

1 tbsp orange juice, plus extra if needed

Honey & Poppy Seed Ring

1. Preheat the oven to 160°C/325°F/Gas Mark 3. Grease a 1.5-litre/2¾-pint Bundt cake tin, preferably non-stick.

2. Sift the flour and baking powder into a large bowl and add the butter, sugar, 4 tablespoons of the honey, the eggs and vanilla extract. Beat well until the mixture is smooth. Stir in the poppy seeds and lemon juice.

3. Spoon the mixture into the prepared tin and smooth the surface with a palette knife. Bake in the preheated oven for 40–50 minutes, or until risen, firm and golden brown.

4. Leave to cool in the tin for 20 minutes, then turn out carefully and finish cooling on a wire rack. To serve, warm the remaining 2 tablespoons of the honey and drizzle over the cake, then cut into slices and serve.

Serves 8–10

* oil or melted butter, for greasing
* 175 g/6 oz plain white flour
* 1 tbsp baking powder
* 175 g/6 oz unsalted butter, softened
* 100 g/3½ oz golden caster sugar
* 6 tbsp clear honey
* 3 eggs, beaten
* 1 tsp vanilla extract
* 30 g/1 oz poppy seeds
* 2 tbsp lemon juice

Lemon Drizzle Loaf

1. Preheat the oven to 180°C/350°F/Gas Mark 4. Grease and line a 1.2-litre/2-pint loaf tin.

2. Sift the flour and baking powder into a large bowl and add the butter, caster sugar, eggs and egg yolk. Beat well until the mixture is smooth, then stir in the lemon rind and juice.

3. Spoon the mixture into the prepared tin and smooth the surface with a palette knife. Bake in the preheated oven for 40–50 minutes, or until well risen, firm and golden brown.

4. Remove the tin from the oven and transfer to a wire rack. For the syrup, place the icing sugar and lemon juice in a saucepan and heat gently without boiling, stirring until the sugar dissolves.

5. Prick the top of the loaf several times with a skewer and spoon over the syrup. Leave to cool completely in the tin, then turn out, scatter with strips of lemon zest and cut into slices.

Serves 8–10

* oil or melted butter, for greasing
* 175 g/6 oz plain white flour
* 1 tbsp baking powder
* 175 g/6 oz unsalted butter, softened
* 175 g/6 oz golden caster sugar
* 3 eggs, beaten
  1 egg yolk
  finely grated rind of 1 lemon
* 2 tbsp lemon juice
  fine strips of lemon zest, to decorate

Syrup
85 g/3 oz icing sugar
3 tbsp lemon juice

15

Hazelnut Crumble Bars

1. Preheat the oven to 160°C/325°F/Gas Mark 3. Grease and line a 20 x 30-cm/8 x 12-inch rectangular cake tin.

2. Sift the flour and baking powder into a large bowl and add the butter, muscovado sugar, eggs, vanilla extract and chocolate spread. Beat well until the mixture is smooth. Stir in the hazelnuts.

3. Spoon the mixture into the prepared tin and smooth the surface with a palette knife. For the topping, mix the flour and chocolate spread to make a crumbly texture, then stir in the demerara sugar and hazelnuts. Spread over the cake mixture.

4. Bake in the preheated oven for 40–50 minutes, or until risen and firm. Leave to cool in the tin before cutting into bars.

Makes 12–16

* oil or melted butter, for greasing
* 175 g/6 oz plain white flour
* 2 tsp baking powder
* 115 g/4 oz unsalted butter, softened
* 175 g/6 oz light muscovado sugar
* 3 eggs, beaten
* 1 tsp vanilla extract
* 55 g/2 oz chocolate hazelnut spread
* 55 g/2 oz hazelnuts, chopped

Topping
50 g/1¾ oz plain white flour
55 g/2 oz chocolate hazelnut spread
2 tbsp demerara sugar
40 g/1½ oz hazelnuts, chopped

Apple Sauce Cake

1. Preheat the oven to 180°C/350°F/Gas Mark 4. Grease two 20-cm/8-inch sandwich cake tins and line the bases with baking paper.

2. Sift the flour, cornflour and baking powder into a large bowl and add the butter, sugar, eggs and vanilla extract. Beat well until the mixture is smooth. Stir in 85 g/3 oz of the apple sauce.

3. Divide the mixture between the prepared tins and smooth the surfaces with a palette knife. Bake in the preheated oven for 25–30 minutes, or until risen, firm and golden brown.

4. Leave to cool in the tins for 5 minutes, then turn out carefully and finish cooling on a wire rack. Use the remaining apple sauce to sandwich the cakes together.

5. Core and thinly slice the apple and brush with lemon juice. Arrange the slices on top of the cake to decorate, then sprinkle with a little caster sugar.

Serves 6

- oil or melted butter, for greasing
- 175 g/6 oz plain white flour
- 1 tbsp cornflour
- 1 tbsp baking powder
- 175 g/6 oz unsalted butter, softened
- 175 g/6 oz caster sugar, plus extra for sprinkling
- 3 eggs, beaten
- 1 tsp vanilla extract
- 200 g/7 oz apple sauce or thick apple purée
- 1 eating apple
- lemon juice, for brushing

17

Prune & Walnut Swirl Cake

1. Preheat the oven to 160°C/325°F/Gas Mark 3. Grease and line a 19-cm/7½-inch square deep cake tin.

2. Place the prunes in a pan with the apple juice, bring to the boil, then reduce the heat and simmer for 8–10 minutes, until the liquid is absorbed. Process the prune mixture in a food processor or blender to a smooth, thick purée.

3. Sift the flour and baking powder into a large bowl and add the butter, sugar, eggs and vanilla extract. Beat well until the mixture is smooth. Reserve 2 tablespoons of the walnuts, then stir the remainder into the cake mixture.

4. Spoon the mixture into the prepared tin, then drop spoonfuls of the prune purée over the top. Swirl into the cake mix with a knife and smooth the surface level. Scatter the reserved walnuts over the cake.

5. Bake in the preheated oven for 1 hour–1 hour 10 minutes, or until risen, firm and golden brown. Leave to cool in the tin for 10 minutes, then turn out and finish cooling on a wire rack. Cut into squares to serve.

Serves 12

* oil or melted butter, for greasing
* 200 g/7 oz ready-to-eat pitted prunes
* 150 ml/5 fl oz apple juice
* 200 g/7 oz plain white flour
* 2 tsp baking powder
* 175 g/6 oz unsalted butter, softened
* 175 g/6 oz golden caster sugar
* 3 eggs, beaten
* 1 tsp vanilla extract
* 70 g/2½ oz walnuts, roughly chopped

Coconut Lamingtons

1. Preheat the oven to 180°C/350°F/Gas Mark 4. Grease and line a 23-cm/9-inch square cake tin.

2. Sift the flour and baking powder into a large bowl and add the butter, caster sugar, eggs and vanilla extract. Beat well until the mixture is smooth, then stir in the milk and coconut.

3. Spoon the mixture into the prepared tin and smooth the surface with a palette knife. Bake in the preheated oven for 30–35 minutes, or until risen, firm and golden brown.

4. Leave to cool in the tin for 10 minutes, then turn out and finish cooling on a wire rack. When the cake is cold, cut into 16 squares with a sharp knife.

5. For the icing, sift the icing sugar and cocoa into a bowl. Add the water and butter and stir until smooth. Spread out the coconut on a large plate. Dip each piece of sponge cake into the icing, holding with two forks to coat evenly, then toss in coconut to cover.

6. Place on a sheet of baking paper and leave to set.

Makes 16

* oil or melted butter, for greasing
* 175 g/6 oz plain white flour
* 1 tbsp baking powder
* 175 g/6 oz unsalted butter, softened
* 175 g/6 oz caster sugar
* 3 eggs, beaten
* 1 tsp vanilla extract
* 2 tbsp milk
  2 tbsp desiccated coconut

Icing and coating
500 g/1 lb 2 oz icing sugar
40 g/1½ oz cocoa powder
85 ml/3 fl oz boiling water
70 g/2½ oz unsalted butter, melted
250 g/9 oz desiccated coconut

Marshmallow Crunch Bars

1. Preheat the oven to 180°C/350°F/Gas Mark 4. Grease and line a 23-cm/9-inch square cake tin.

2. Sift the flour and baking powder into a large bowl and add the butter, sugar, eggs and vanilla extract. Beat well until the mixture is smooth. Stir about two thirds of the nuts and glacé cherries into the mixture.

3. Spoon the mixture into the prepared tin and smooth level with a palette knife. Scatter the remaining nuts and glacé cherries and the marshmallows over the top, pressing down lightly.

4. Bake in the preheated oven for 40–50 minutes, or until risen and golden brown.

5. Leave to cool in the tin for about 20 minutes, until firm, then cut into bars and finish cooling on a wire rack.

Makes 8

* oil or melted butter, for greasing
* 175 g/6 oz plain white flour
* 1 tbsp baking powder
* 175 g/6 oz unsalted butter, softened
* 175 g/6 oz caster sugar
* 3 eggs, beaten
* 1 tsp vanilla extract
* 100 g/3½ oz chopped mixed nuts
* 85 g/3 oz glacé cherries, roughly chopped
* 55 g/2 oz mini marshmallows

20

Cherry Almond Slices

1. Preheat the oven to 190°C/375°F/Gas Mark 5. Grease and line an 18 x 28-cm/7 x 11-inch rectangular cake tin.

2. Sift the flour and baking powder into a bowl and add the butter, sugar, eggs and almond extract. Stir in the lemon rind, ground almonds and half the glacé cherries.

3. Spoon the mixture into the prepared tin, smoothing level with a palette knife. Sprinkle the remaining glacé cherries and the flaked almonds over the mixture.

4. Bake in the preheated oven for 40–50 minutes, until risen, firm and golden brown. Leave to cool in the tin, then cut into slices to serve.

Makes 8

oil or melted butter, for greasing

115 g/4 oz plain white flour

2 tsp baking powder

175 g/6 oz unsalted butter, softened

175 g/6 oz golden caster sugar

3 eggs, beaten

1 tsp almond extract

finely grated rind of 1 lemon

115 g/4 oz ground almonds

140 g/5 oz glacé cherries, chopped

30 g/1 oz flaked almonds

Special

21

White Chocolate Valentine's Gateau

1. Preheat the oven to 160°C/325°F/Gas Mark 3. Grease a 1.5-litre/2¾-pint heart-shaped cake tin.

2. Sift the flour and baking powder into a bowl and add the butter, sugar, eggs and vanilla extract. Beat well until smooth, then stir in the grated chocolate.

3. Spoon the mixture into the prepared tin and smooth the surface with a palette knife. Bake in the preheated oven for 45–55 minutes, or until risen, firm and golden brown. Leave to cool in the tin for 10 minutes, then turn out onto a wire rack to finish cooling.

4. For the frosting, melt the chocolate with the milk in a heatproof bowl set over a pan of hot water. Remove from the heat and stir until smooth, then leave to cool for 10 minutes. Whip the cream until it holds soft peaks, then fold into the cooled chocolate mixture.

5. Sprinkle the cake with the rum, if using. Spread the frosting over the top and sides of the cake, swirling with a palette knife, then decorate with crystallized violets.

Serves 10

- oil or melted butter, for greasing
- 175 g/6 oz plain white flour
- 1 tbsp baking powder
- 175 g/6 oz unsalted butter, softened
- 175 g/6 oz caster sugar
- 3 eggs, beaten
- 1 tsp vanilla extract
- 55 g/2 oz white chocolate, grated
- 2 tbsp white rum (optional)
- crystallized violets, to decorate

Frosting
200 g/7 oz white chocolate, broken into pieces
2 tbsp milk
200 ml/7 fl oz double cream

22

Halloween Pumpkin Cake

1. Preheat the oven to 160°C/325°F/Gas Mark 3. Grease and line a 23-cm/9-inch round deep cake tin.

2. Sift the flour, baking powder and mixed spice into a bowl and add the butter, sugar, eggs and vanilla extract. Beat well until smooth, then stir in the pumpkin.

3. Spoon the mixture into the prepared tin and spread the top level. Bake in the preheated oven for 40–50 minutes, or until risen, firm and golden brown. Leave to cool in the tin for 10 minutes, then turn out onto a wire rack to finish cooling.

4. Brush the cake with warmed apricot jam. Knead orange food colouring into about three quarters of the icing and roll out to cover the top and sides of the cake. Trim the edges neatly, reserving the trimmings.

5. Form the trimmings into small pumpkin shapes and use the black writing icing to pipe faces and the green writing icing to pipe stalks onto them. Knead black food colouring into the remaining icing, then roll it out and cut into bat shapes. Pipe eyes onto the bats using yellow writing icing, then place the bats and the pumpkins onto the cake to decorate.

Serves 10

* oil or melted butter, for greasing
* 175 g/6 oz plain white flour
* 1 tbsp baking powder
* 1 tsp ground mixed spice
* 175 g/6 oz unsalted butter, softened
* 175 g/6 oz light muscovado sugar
* 3 eggs, beaten
* 1 tsp vanilla extract
* 175 g/6 oz pumpkin flesh, coarsely grated

To decorate
3 tbsp apricot jam, warmed

a few drops of orange and black edible food colouring

800 g/1 lb 12 oz ready-to-roll soft icing

black, green and yellow writing icing

Birthday Number Cake

1. Preheat the oven to 160°C/325°F/Gas Mark 3. Grease and line a 25 x 18-cm/10 x 7-inch numeral cake tin or a frame on a baking sheet, about 5 cm/2 inches deep.

2. Sift the flour and baking powder into a large bowl and add the butter, caster sugar, eggs and vanilla extract. Beat well until the mixture is smooth, then stir in the orange juice and rind.

3. Spoon the mixture into the prepared tin and smooth the surface with a palette knife. Bake in the preheated oven for 40–50 minutes, or until risen, firm and golden brown. Leave to cool in the tin for 5 minutes, then turn out and finish cooling on a wire rack.

4. For the frosting, beat together the icing sugar, butter, orange rind and juice until smooth. Spread over the cake evenly, smoothing with a palette knife.

5. Arrange the orange slices on top of the cake to decorate, then add the birthday candles and serve.

Serves 10–12

- oil or melted butter, for greasing
- 175 g/6 oz plain white flour
- 1 tbsp baking powder
- 175 g/6 oz unsalted butter, softened
- 175 g/6 oz caster sugar
- 3 eggs, beaten
- 1 tsp vanilla extract
- 2 tbsp orange juice
  finely grated rind of ½ orange
  sugar orange slices and birthday candles, to decorate

Frosting
350 g/12 oz icing sugar, sifted
175 g/6 oz unsalted butter, softened
finely grated rind of ½ orange
1 tbsp orange juice

Bumblebee Cake

1. Preheat the oven to 160°C/325°F/Gas Mark 3. Grease a 1.5-litre/2¾-pint ovenproof pudding basin.

2. Sift the flour and baking powder into a bowl and add the butter, caster sugar, eggs and vanilla extract. Beat well until smooth, then stir in the lemon juice and rind.

3. Spoon the mixture into the prepared basin and spread the top level. Bake in the preheated oven for 1¼–1½ hours, or until risen, firm and golden brown. Leave to cool in the basin for 5 minutes, then turn out onto a wire rack to finish cooling.

4. For the frosting, beat together the butter, icing sugar, honey and lemon juice until smooth. Slice the cake horizontally into three layers. Use about a quarter of the frosting to sandwich the layers together.

5. Using a piping bag with a large plain nozzle, pipe the remaining frosting in lines around the cake to resemble a beehive.

6. Reserve a quarter of the white icing, then colour half the remainder yellow and half black. Shape to make small bees, making the wings from the white icing and fixing with a dab of water. Press the bees into the frosting.

Serves 8–10

oil or melted butter, for greasing

235 g/8½ oz plain white flour

1 tbsp baking powder

175 g/6 oz unsalted butter, softened

175 g/6 oz caster sugar

3 eggs, beaten

1 tsp vanilla extract

2 tbsp lemon juice

finely grated rind of 1 lemon

Frosting

175 g/6 oz unsalted butter

250 g/9 oz icing sugar, sifted

3 tbsp clear honey

2 tbsp lemon juice

To decorate

250 g/9 oz white ready-to-roll icing

a few drops of yellow and black edible food colouring

25

Rich Chocolate Rum Torte

1. Preheat the oven to 180°C/350°F/Gas Mark 4. Grease and line three 18-cm/7-inch sandwich cake tins.

2. Place the chocolate and milk in a small saucepan and heat gently, without boiling, until melted. Stir and remove from the heat.

3. Sift the flour and baking powder into a large bowl and add the butter, sugar, eggs and vanilla extract. Beat well until smooth, then stir in the chocolate mixture.

4. Divide the mixture between the prepared tins and smooth the surfaces with a palette knife. Bake in the preheated oven for 20–25 minutes, until risen and firm to the touch.

5. Leave to cool in the tins for 5 minutes, then turn out and finish cooling on wire racks.

6. For the frosting, melt the chocolate with the cream and rum in a small saucepan over a low heat. Remove from the heat and leave to cool, stirring occasionally, until it reaches a spreadable consistency.

7. Sandwich the cakes together with about a third of the frosting, then spread the remainder over the top and sides of the cake, swirling with a palette knife. Sprinkle with chocolate curls or grated chocolate and leave to set.

Serves 8

- oil or melted butter, for greasing
- 70 g/2½ oz plain chocolate, broken into pieces
- 2 tbsp milk
- 175 g/6 oz plain white flour
- 1 tbsp baking powder
- 175 g/6 oz unsalted butter, softened
- 175 g/6 oz dark muscovado sugar
- 3 eggs, beaten
- 1 tsp vanilla extract
- chocolate curls or grated chocolate, to decorate

Frosting
225 g/8 oz plain chocolate, broken into pieces
225 ml/8 fl oz double cream
2 tbsp dark rum

Orange Cheesecake Gateau

1. Preheat the oven to 180°C/350°F/Gas Mark 4. Grease and line two 23-cm/9-inch sandwich cake tins.

2. Sift the flour and baking powder into a large bowl and add the butter, caster sugar, eggs and orange flower water. Beat well until the mixture is smooth, then stir in the orange juice.

3. Spoon the mixture into the prepared tins and smooth the surfaces with a palette knife. Bake in the preheated oven for 25–30 minutes, or until risen and golden brown. Leave to cool in the tins for 5 minutes, then turn out and finish cooling on a wire rack.

4. Beat together all the filling ingredients until smooth, then spread about a third over one cake. Spoon the remainder into a piping bag fitted with a large star nozzle and pipe swirls around the edge of the cake.

5. Place the second cake on top. Pipe the remaining frosting around the top edge. Fill the centre with orange slices and brush with maple syrup.

Serves 8–10

* oil or melted butter, for greasing
* 175 g/6 oz plain white flour
* 1 tbsp baking powder
* 175 g/6 oz unsalted butter, softened
* 175 g/6 oz golden caster sugar
* 3 eggs, beaten
* 1 tsp orange flower water
* 2 tbsp orange juice

Filling
600 g/1 lb 5 oz mascarpone cheese
finely grated rind of 1 orange
4 tbsp orange juice
55 g/2 oz icing sugar
1 tsp orange flower water

Topping
1 orange, peeled and sliced
maple syrup, for brushing

Sweetie Birthday Cake

1. Preheat the oven to 160°C/325°F/Gas Mark 3. Grease and line two 20 cm/8-inch square sandwich cake tins.

2. Sift the flour and baking powder into a large bowl and add the butter, sugar, eggs and vanilla extract. Beat well until the mixture is smooth, then stir in the milk.

3. Divide the mixture between the prepared tins and smooth the surfaces with a palette knife. Bake in the preheated oven for 25–30 minutes, or until risen, firm and golden brown. Leave to cool in the tins for 2–3 minutes, then turn out and finish cooling on a wire rack.

4. Warm the apricot jam with the lemon juice in a small pan until melted. Spread half over one cake and place the other cake on top. Brush the remaining jam over the top and sides of the cakes.

5. Roll out the icing to cover the cakes, smoothing with your hands, then trim the edges with a sharp knife. Decorate with sweets and birthday candles.

Serves 8–10

- oil or melted butter, for greasing
- 175 g/6 oz plain white flour
- 1 tbsp baking powder
- 175 g/6 oz unsalted butter, softened
- 175 g/6 oz golden caster sugar
- 3 eggs, beaten
- 1 tsp vanilla extract
- 2 tbsp milk
- coloured sweets and birthday candles, to decorate

Filling and topping
5 tbsp apricot jam
1 tbsp lemon juice
500 g/1 lb 2 oz ready-to-roll soft icing

28

Frosted Raspberry Almond Ring

1. Preheat the oven to 160°C/325°F/Gas Mark 3. Grease a 1.5-litre/2¾-pint ring cake tin, preferably non-stick.

2. Sift the flour and baking powder into a large bowl and add the butter, caster sugar, eggs and almond extract. Beat well until the mixture is smooth, then stir in the ground almonds. Mash half the raspberries with a fork and stir into the mixture.

3. Spoon the mixture into the prepared tin and smooth the surface with a palette knife. Bake in the preheated oven for 40–45 minutes, or until risen, firm and golden brown.

4. Leave to cool in the tin for 10 minutes, then turn out carefully onto a wire rack to finish cooling.

5. For the frosting, place the egg white, icing sugar, golden syrup and cream of tartar in a bowl over a saucepan of hot water and whisk vigorously with a hand-held electric mixer until thick enough to hold its shape.

6. Swirl the frosting over the top of the cake. Decorate with the remaining raspberries and the flaked almonds.

Serves 8–10

* oil or melted butter, for greasing
* 175 g/6 oz plain white flour
* 1 tbsp baking powder
* 175 g/6 oz unsalted butter, softened
* 175 g/6 oz caster sugar
* 3 eggs, beaten
* 1 tsp almond extract
  70 g/2½ oz ground almonds
  225 g/8 oz fresh raspberries
  toasted flaked almonds, to decorate

Frosting
1 large egg white
140 g/5 oz icing sugar
1 tbsp golden syrup
¼ tsp cream of tartar

Glazed Fruit & Nut Cake

1. Preheat the oven to 160°C/325°F/Gas Mark 3. Grease a 23-cm/9-inch round spring-release cake tin and sprinkle with a little flour to coat, shaking out the excess.

2. Sift the flour, baking powder and mixed spice into a large bowl and add the butter, sugar, eggs and vanilla extract. Beat well until the mixture is smooth, then stir in the milk, mixed dried fruit and chopped mixed nuts.

3. Spoon the mixture into the prepared tin and smooth the surface with a palette knife. Bake in the preheated oven for about 1 hour, or until risen, firm and golden brown.

4. Leave to cool in the tin for 30 minutes, then remove the sides and place on a wire rack to finish cooling.

5. Brush the top of the cake with a little of the warmed honey then arrange the glacé fruits and whole shelled nuts on top. Brush with the remaining honey and leave to set.

Serves 16–18

- oil or melted butter, for greasing
- 250 g/9 oz plain white flour, plus extra for sprinkling
- 1 tbsp baking powder
- 1 tsp ground mixed spice
- 175 g/6 oz unsalted butter, softened
- 175 g/6 oz dark muscovado sugar
- 3 eggs, beaten
- 1 tsp vanilla extract
- 2 tbsp milk
- 300 g/10½ oz mixed dried fruit
- 85 g/3 oz chopped mixed nuts

To decorate

- 3 tbsp clear honey, warmed
- 350 g/12 oz mixed glacé fruits, such as pineapple, cherries and orange
- 55 g/2 oz whole shelled nuts, such as Brazil nuts, almonds and walnuts

Rose Gateau

1. Preheat the oven to 180°C/350°F/Gas Mark 4. Grease two 23-cm/9-inch sandwich cake tins and line the bases with baking paper.

2. Sift the flour and baking powder into a large bowl and add the butter, caster sugar, eggs and rosewater. Beat well until the mixture is smooth, then stir in the milk.

3. Divide the mixture between the prepared tins and smooth the surfaces with a palette knife. Bake in the preheated oven for 25–30 minutes, or until risen, firm and golden brown. Leave to cool in the tins for 2–3 minutes, then turn out and finish cooling on a wire rack.

4. Whip the cream with ½ teaspoon of the rosewater until just thick enough to hold its shape. Use to sandwich the cakes together.

5. For the icing, mix the icing sugar with the remaining rosewater and just enough water to mix to a thick pouring consistency. Spoon over the cake, allowing it to drizzle down the sides. Leave to set.

6. Brush the rose petals with the egg white, sprinkle with caster sugar and arrange on top of the cake to decorate.

Serves 8–10

* oil or melted butter, for greasing
* 175 g/6 oz plain white flour
* 1 tbsp baking powder
* 175 g/6 oz unsalted butter, softened
* 175 g/6 oz caster sugar
* 3 eggs, beaten
* 1 tsp rosewater
* 2 tbsp milk

Filling and icing
150 ml/5 fl oz whipping cream
1 tsp rosewater
200 g/7 oz icing sugar, sifted

To decorate
fresh rose petals, washed and patted dry
½ egg white
caster sugar, for sprinkling

31

Christmas Mulled Sponge Loaf

1. Preheat the oven to 180°C/350°F/Gas Mark 4. Grease and line a 1.2-litre/2-pint loaf tin.

2. Sift the flour, baking powder and mixed spice into a large bowl and add the butter, muscovado sugar, eggs and vanilla extract. Beat well until the mixture is smooth, then stir in the orange rind and juice.

3. Spoon the mixture into the prepared tin and smooth level with a palette knife. Bake in the preheated oven for 40–50 minutes, or until risen, firm and golden brown. (Don't worry if the cake dips slightly in the centre.)

4. Remove the tin from the oven and stand it on a wire rack. To make the syrup, place the icing sugar, port and star anise in a pan and heat gently until boiling. Boil rapidly for 2–3 minutes to reduce slightly. Remove and discard the star anise.

5. Spoon the syrup over the cake and leave to soak for 30 minutes. Turn out the cake from the tin, upside down.

6. Brush the cranberries and bay leaves with egg white and sprinkle with caster sugar, then arrange on top of the cake.

Serves 8

- oil or melted butter, for greasing
- 175 g/6 oz plain white flour
- 1 tbsp baking powder
- 1 tsp ground mixed spice
- 175 g/6 oz unsalted butter, softened
- 175 g/6 oz light muscovado sugar
- 3 eggs, beaten
- 1 tsp vanilla extract
- finely grated rind of 1 orange
- 2 tbsp orange juice

Syrup
70 g/2½ oz icing sugar
100 ml/3½ fl oz port or red wine
1 piece star anise

To decorate
10 fresh cranberries
10 fresh bay leaves
1 egg white
caster sugar, for sprinkling

Silver Wedding Anniversary Cake

1. Preheat the oven to 180°C/350°F/Gas Mark 4. Grease a 18-cm/7-inch sandwich cake tin and a 23-cm/9-inch sandwich cake tin and line the bases with baking paper.

2. Sift the flour and baking powder into a large bowl and add the butter, caster sugar, eggs and vanilla extract. Beat well until the mixture is smooth, then stir in the milk.

3. Spoon the mixture into the prepared tins and smooth the surfaces with a palette knife. Bake in the preheated oven for 20–25 minutes for the small cake and 25–30 minutes for the large cake, or until risen, firm and golden brown.

4. Leave to cool in the tins for 2–3 minutes, then turn out and finish cooling on wire racks. Prick the cakes with a skewer and sprinkle with the sherry.

5. For the frosting, beat together the mascarpone, cream and icing sugar to a smooth, spreading consistency, adding a little more icing sugar if needed. Spread a little frosting on top of the centre of the larger cake, then place the small cake on top, pressing down lightly.

6. Spread the remaining frosting over the cakes, swirling with a palette knife, then decorate with silver balls.

Serves 10–12

* oil or melted butter, for greasing
* 175 g/6 oz plain white flour
* 1 tbsp baking powder
* 175 g/6 oz unsalted butter, softened
* 175 g/6 oz caster sugar
* 3 eggs, beaten
* 1 tsp vanilla extract
* 2 tbsp milk
  2 tbsp medium sherry
  silver balls, to decorate

Frosting
250 g/9 oz mascarpone cheese
3 tbsp single cream
500 g/1 lb 2 oz icing sugar, sifted, plus extra if needed

Easter Cake

1. Preheat the oven to 160°C/325°F/Gas Mark 3. Grease and line a 23-cm/9-inch square cake tin.

2. Sift the flour, baking powder and mixed spice into a large bowl and add the butter, sugar, eggs and almond extract. Beat well until the mixture is smooth, then stir in the milk, ground almonds and mixed dried fruit.

3. Spoon the mixture into the tin and smooth the surface with a palette knife. Bake in the preheated oven for 1–1¼ hours, or until risen, firm and golden brown. Leave to cool in the tin for 30 minutes, then turn out onto a wire rack to finish cooling.

4. Brush the top of the cake with the warmed apricot jam. Roll out about half the marzipan and use to cover the cake top, trimming the edges neatly. Score the top lightly with a knife in a diamond pattern.

5. Roll the remaining marzipan into 12 thin ropes, each about 25 cm/10 inches long, and plait together in threes. Arrange 1 plait along each top edge of the cake, trimming the ends.

6. Preheat the grill to high. Lightly brush the marzipan with egg white, then grill the cake for 3–4 minutes, or until golden brown on top. Leave to cool before serving.

Serves 16

oil or melted butter, for greasing

225 g/8 oz plain white flour

2½ tsp baking powder

1 tsp ground mixed spice

175 g/6 oz unsalted butter, softened

175 g/6 oz light muscovado sugar

3 eggs, beaten

1 tsp almond extract

2 tbsp milk

85 g/3 oz ground almonds

350 g/12 oz mixed dried fruit

To decorate

2 tbsp apricot jam, warmed

900 g/2 lb golden marzipan

egg white, for brushing

34

Walnut Torte

1. Preheat the oven to 180°C/350°F/Gas Mark 4. Grease two 20-cm/8-inch sandwich cake tins and line the bases with baking paper.

2. Sift the flour and baking powder into a large bowl and add the butter, caster sugar, eggs and vanilla extract. Beat well until the mixture is smooth, then stir in the milk and 40 g/1½ oz of the chopped walnuts.

3. Divide the mixture between the prepared tins and smooth the surfaces with a palette knife. Bake in the preheated oven for 25–30 minutes, or until risen, firm and golden brown.

4. Leave to cool in the tins for 2–3 minutes, then turn out and finish cooling on a wire rack. Slice each cake in half horizontally, to make four layers in total.

5. For the frosting, beat together the butter, icing sugar and cream until smooth. Spread about half the frosting over the top of three of the cakes and sandwich them together, placing the plain one on top.

6. Spread half the remaining frosting over the sides of the cake to cover thinly and press the remaining chopped walnuts over it. Brush the apricot jam over the top of the cake. Spoon the remaining frosting into a piping bag fitted with a star nozzle and pipe swirls of frosting around the top edge of the cake. Decorate the top with walnut halves.

Serves 8–10

* oil or melted butter, for greasing
* 175 g/6 oz plain white flour
* 1 tbsp baking powder
* 175 g/6 oz unsalted butter, softened
* 175 g/6 oz golden caster sugar
* 3 eggs, beaten
* 1 tsp vanilla extract
* 2 tbsp milk
  125 g/4½ oz walnuts, finely chopped, plus extra walnut halves to decorate
  3 tbsp apricot jam, warmed

Frosting
175 g/6 oz unsalted butter
350 g/12 oz icing sugar, sifted
100 ml/3½ fl oz single cream

Meringue-topped Coffee Liqueur Cake

1. Preheat the oven to 160°C/325°F/Gas Mark 3. Grease and line a 25-cm/10-inch round cake tin.

2. Sift the flour and baking powder into a large bowl and add the butter, muscovado sugar, eggs and coffee extract. Beat well until the mixture is smooth, then stir in the milk.

3. Spoon the mixture into the prepared tin and smooth the surface with a palette knife. Bake in the preheated oven for 40–50 minutes, or until risen, firm and golden brown.

4. Leave to cool in the tin for 2–3 minutes, then turn out onto a flameproof serving plate. Prick the cake all over with a skewer, then sprinkle with the liqueur.

5. For the meringue topping, place the egg whites in a clean bowl and whisk with a hand-held electric mixer until thick enough to hold soft peaks. Gradually add the caster sugar, whisking vigorously after each addition, then whisk in the coffee extract.

6. Spoon the meringue on top of the cake and spread into peaks and swirls with a palette knife. Use a chef's blowtorch to brown the meringue or place the cake under a hot grill for 2–3 minutes, or until just browned but still soft inside. Cut into slices and serve.

Serves 6–8

- oil or melted butter, for greasing
- 175 g/6 oz plain white flour
- 1 tbsp baking powder
- 175 g/6 oz unsalted butter, softened
- 175 g/6 oz light muscovado sugar
- 3 eggs, beaten
- 1 tsp coffee extract
- 2 tbsp milk
- 3 tbsp coffee liqueur

Meringue topping
3 egg whites
150 g/5½ oz caster sugar
1½ tsp coffee extract

36

Strawberry Mousse Cake

1. Preheat the oven to 160°C/325°F/Gas Mark 3. Grease and line a 23 cm/9-inch round spring-release cake tin.

2. Sift the flour and baking powder into a large bowl and add the butter, sugar, eggs and vanilla extract. Beat well until the mixture is smooth, then stir in the milk.

3. Spoon the mixture into the prepared tin and smooth the surface with a palette knife. Bake in the preheated oven for 45–55 minutes, or until risen, firm and golden brown.

4. Leave to cool in the tin for 5 minutes, then turn out and finish cooling on a wire rack. Cut the sponge in half horizontally and place one half back in the cake tin.

5. For the filling, dissolve the gelatine in the orange juice in a small bowl placed in a saucepan of hot water. In a blender or processor, purée 400 g/14 oz of the strawberries with the sugar. Whip the cream until thick enough to hold its shape. Quickly stir the gelatine mixture into the strawberry mixture, then fold in the cream.

6. Pour the mixture into the tin and place the second half of the cake on top. Chill in the refrigerator until set. Turn out the cake and spread the top with the warmed redcurrant jelly. Decorate with the remaining strawberries.

Serves 8–10

* oil or melted butter, for greasing
* 175 g/6 oz plain white flour
* 1 tbsp baking powder
* 175 g/6 oz unsalted butter, softened
* 175 g/6 oz golden caster sugar
* 3 eggs, beaten
* 1 tsp vanilla extract
* 2 tbsp milk

Filling and topping

4 tsp powdered gelatine

3 tbsp orange juice

550 g/1 lb 4 oz fresh strawberries

3 tbsp golden caster sugar

400 ml/14 fl oz double cream

100 g/3½ oz redcurrant jelly, warmed

37

Lemon & Pistachio Ring

1. Preheat the oven to 180°C/350°F/Gas Mark 4. Grease a 1.5-litre/2¾-pint Bundt cake tin.

2. Sift the flour and baking powder into a large bowl and add the butter, sugar, eggs and lemon extract. Beat well until the mixture is smooth, then stir in the lemon rind, lemon juice and finely chopped pistachio nuts.

3. Spoon the mixture into the prepared tin and smooth the surface with a palette knife. Bake in the preheated oven for 40–50 minutes, or until risen, firm and golden brown.

4. Leave to cool in the tin for 10 minutes, then turn out onto a wire rack to finish cooling.

5. To decorate, thinly pare the zest from the lemon. Cut into long, thin strips and place in a pan with the sugar and water. Heat gently until the sugar dissolves, then bring to the boil and boil for 7 minutes. Remove the strips of zest from the syrup and leave to cool on a sheet of baking paper.

6. Arrange the crystallized lemon strips over the cake and scatter with the roughly chopped pistachio nuts.

Serves 10

- oil or melted butter, for greasing
- 175 g/6 oz plain white flour
- 2 tsp baking powder
- 175 g/6 oz unsalted butter, softened
- 175 g/6 oz caster sugar
- 3 eggs, beaten
- 1 tsp lemon extract
- finely grated rind of 1 lemon
- 1 tbsp lemon juice
- 40 g/1½ oz pistachio nuts, finely chopped

To decorate
- 1 lemon
- 85 g/3 oz caster sugar
- 50 ml/2 fl oz water
- 2 tbsp roughly chopped pistachio nuts

38

Blueberry Swirl Gateau

1. Preheat the oven to 160°C/325°F/Gas Mark 3. Grease three 19-cm/7½-inch sandwich cake tins and line the bases with baking paper.

2. Sift the flour and baking powder into a large bowl and add the butter, caster sugar, eggs and orange flower water. Beat well until the mixture is smooth, then stir in the orange juice.

3. Spoon the mixture into the prepared tins and smooth the surfaces with a palette knife. Bake in the preheated oven for 20–25 minutes, or until risen, firm and golden brown.

4. Leave to cool in the tins for 2–3 minutes, then turn out and finish cooling on a wire rack.

5. For the frosting, beat together the soft cheese and icing sugar until smooth. Transfer about two thirds of the mixture to a separate bowl and stir in 140 g/5 oz of the blueberries, then use this to sandwich the cakes together.

6. Rub the remaining blueberries through a fine sieve to make a smooth purée. Spread the remaining frosting on top of the cake and swirl the blueberry purée through it.

Serves 8–10

- oil or melted butter, for greasing
- 175 g/6 oz plain white flour
- 1 tbsp baking powder
- 175 g/6 oz unsalted butter, softened
- 175 g/6 oz caster sugar
- 3 eggs, beaten
- 1 tsp orange flower water
- 2 tbsp orange juice

Filling and frosting
200 g/7 oz full-fat soft cheese
100 g/3½ oz icing sugar, sifted
225 g/8 oz fresh blueberries

Caramel Sponge Layer

1. Preheat the oven to 180°C/350°F/Gas Mark 4. Grease and line a 23-cm/9-inch square cake tin.

2. Sift the flour and baking powder into a large bowl and add the butter, muscovado sugar, eggs and vanilla extract. Beat well until the mixture is smooth, then stir in the milk.

3. Spoon into the prepared tin and smooth the surface level. Bake in the preheated oven for 35–40 minutes, or until risen, firm and golden brown.

4. Leave to cool in the tin for 5 minutes, then turn out and finish cooling on a wire rack. Slice the cake horizontally into two layers.

5. For the frosting, heat the golden syrup in a pan until very hot. Gradually pour into the egg yolks, whisking hard until the mixture is pale and thick. Whisk in the butter and vanilla extract to make a glossy frosting. Cover and leave until cold.

6. Heat the caster sugar in a heavy-based pan over a low heat until melted. Boil to a rich, golden caramel. Immediately pour onto a greased baking sheet. Leave to set.

7. Crush half the caramel finely, stir into half the frosting and use to sandwich the cakes together. Spread the remaining frosting on top. Break the remaining caramel into small pieces, then scatter on top of the cake to decorate.

Serves 10–12

* oil or melted butter, for greasing
* 175 g/6 oz plain white flour
* 1 tbsp baking powder
* 175 g/6 oz unsalted butter, softened
* 175 g/6 oz light muscovado sugar
* 3 eggs, beaten
* 1 tsp vanilla extract
* 2 tbsp milk

Frosting and decoration
85 g/3 oz golden syrup
2 egg yolks, beaten
175 g/6 oz unsalted butter, softened
1 tsp vanilla extract
175 g/6 oz caster sugar

Marbled Pastel Cake

1. Preheat the oven to 160°C/325°F/Gas Mark 3. Grease and line a 23-cm/9-inch round deep cake tin.

2. Sift the flour and baking powder into a large bowl and add the butter, sugar, eggs and vanilla extract. Beat well until the mixture is smooth, then stir in the milk. Spoon half the mixture into a separate bowl and stir in a few drops of pink food colouring.

3. Spoon alternate tablespoonfuls of the two mixtures into the prepared tin and swirl lightly with a palette knife for a marbled effect.

4. Bake in the preheated oven for 40–50 minutes, or until risen, firm and golden brown. Leave to cool in the tin for 10 minutes, then turn out and finish cooling on a wire rack.

5. Divide the icing into two halves and knead a little pink food colouring into one half. Knead the pink and white icing together for a marbled effect.

6. Place the cake on a board, brush with apricot jam and roll out the icing to cover the cake. Trim the edges, then roll out the trimmings into two long ropes, twist together and place around the base of the cake. Decorate with sugar flowers.

Serves 12

* oil or melted butter, for greasing
* 175 g/6 oz plain white flour
* 1 tbsp baking powder
* 175 g/6 oz unsalted butter, softened
* 175 g/6 oz caster sugar
* 3 eggs, beaten
* 1 tsp vanilla extract
* 2 tbsp milk
  pink edible food colouring
  700 g/1 lb 9 oz ready-to-roll soft icing
  3 tbsp apricot jam, warmed
  sugar flowers, to decorate

Dainty

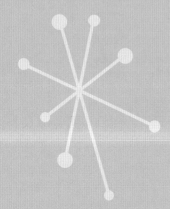

41

Vanilla Hazelnut Yogurt Cupcakes

1. Preheat the oven to 190°C/375°F/Gas Mark 5. Place 26 paper cases into bun tins or put double-layer paper cases onto baking trays.

2. Sift the flour, cornflour and baking powder into a large bowl and add the yogurt, caster sugar, eggs and vanilla extract. Beat well until the mixture is smooth, then stir in the finely chopped hazelnuts.

3. Divide the mixture between the paper cases. Bake in the preheated oven for 15–20 minutes, or until risen, firm and golden brown. Transfer the cupcakes to a wire rack to cool.

4. For the topping, mix the icing sugar and yogurt until smooth, then drizzle over the cupcakes. Scatter over the roughly chopped hazelnuts. Leave to set.

Makes 26

* 175 g/6 oz plain white flour
* 2 tsp cornflour
* 1 tbsp baking powder
* 175 g/6 oz natural yogurt
* 175 g/6 oz golden caster sugar
* 3 eggs, beaten
* 1 tsp vanilla extract
* 40 g/1½ oz hazelnuts, finely chopped

Topping

100 g/3½ oz icing sugar, sifted

40 g/1½ oz natural yogurt

25 g/1 oz hazelnuts, roughly chopped

42

Almond & Apricot Spice Cupcakes

1. Preheat the oven to 190°C/375°F/Gas Mark 5. Place 30 paper cases into bun tins or put double-layer paper cases onto baking trays.

2. Sift the flour, baking powder and allspice into a large bowl and add the butter, sugar, eggs and almond extract. Beat well until the mixture is smooth, then stir in the milk, apricots and ground almonds.

3. Divide the mixture between the paper cases. Bake in the preheated oven for 15–20 minutes, or until risen, firm and golden brown. Transfer the cupcakes to a wire rack to cool.

4. Spoon about a teaspoonful of dulce de leche on top of each cupcake and top with the flaked almonds.

Makes 30

- 175 g/6 oz plain white flour
- 1 tbsp baking powder
- 1 tsp ground allspice
- 175 g/6 oz unsalted butter, softened
- 175 g/6 oz golden caster sugar
- 3 eggs, beaten
- 1 tsp almond extract
- 2 tbsp milk
- 85 g/3 oz ready-to-eat dried apricots, finely chopped
- 40 g/1½ oz ground almonds
- 150 g/5½ oz dulce de leche
- 25 g/1 oz flaked almonds, toasted

43

Maple Pecan Cupcakes

1. Preheat the oven to 190°C/375°F/Gas Mark 5. Place 30 paper cases into bun tins or put double-layer paper cases onto baking trays.

2. Sift the flour and baking powder into a large bowl and add the butter, sugar, maple syrup, eggs and vanilla extract. Beat well until the mixture is smooth, then stir in the pecan nuts.

3. Divide the mixture between the paper cases. For the topping, mix together the pecans, flour, sugar and melted butter to make a crumbly mixture and spoon a little on top of each cupcake.

4. Bake in the preheated oven for 15–20 minutes, or until risen, firm and golden brown. Transfer the cupcakes to a wire rack to cool.

Makes 30

- 175 g/6 oz plain white flour
- 1 tbsp baking powder
- 175 g/6 oz unsalted butter, softened
- 115 g/4 oz light muscovado sugar
- 4 tbsp maple syrup
- 3 eggs, beaten
- 1 tsp vanilla extract
- 30 g/1 oz pecan nuts, finely chopped

Topping
- 40 g/1½ oz pecan nuts, finely chopped
- 2 tbsp plain white flour
- 2 tbsp light muscovado sugar
- 2 tbsp melted butter

Cherry Cupcakes with Ricotta Frosting

1. Preheat the oven to 190°C/375°F/Gas Mark 5. Place 28 paper cases into bun tins or put double-layer paper cases onto baking trays.

2. Stir a tablespoon of the flour into the chopped glacé cherries. Sift the remaining flour with the baking powder and cornflour into a large bowl and add the butter, caster sugar, eggs and vanilla extract. Beat well until the mixture is smooth, then stir in the glacé cherry and flour mixture.

3. Divide the mixture between the paper cases. Bake in the preheated oven for 15–20 minutes, or until risen, firm and golden brown. Transfer the cupcakes to a wire rack to cool.

4. For the frosting, mix the ricotta with the icing sugar and vanilla extract, then spoon a little on top of each cupcake. Top each with half a glacé cherry.

Makes 28

- 175 g/6 oz plain white flour
- 70 g/2½ oz glacé cherries, chopped
- 1 tbsp baking powder
- 1 tbsp cornflour
- 175 g/6 oz unsalted butter, softened
- 175 g/6 oz caster sugar
- 3 eggs, beaten
- 1 tsp vanilla extract
- 14 glacé cherries, halved, to decorate

Frosting
250 g/9 oz ricotta cheese
70 g/2½ oz icing sugar
½ tsp vanilla extract

White Chocolate Chip Cupcakes

1. Preheat the oven to 190°C/375°F/Gas Mark 5. Place 32 paper cases into bun tins or put double-layer paper cases onto baking sheets.

2. Sift the flour and baking powder into a large bowl and add the butter, sugar, eggs and vanilla extract. Beat well until the mixture is smooth, then stir in half the chocolate chips.

3. Divide the mixture between the paper cases and sprinkle with the remaining chocolate chips. Bake in the preheated oven for 15–20 minutes, or until risen, firm and golden brown. Transfer the cupcakes to a wire rack to cool.

4. When the cupcakes are cold, spoon a little melted white chocolate on top of each and scatter over the chocolate sprinkles. Leave to set.

Makes 32

- 175 g/6 oz plain white flour
- 1 tbsp baking powder
- 175 g/6 oz unsalted butter, softened
- 175 g/6 oz golden caster sugar
- 3 eggs, beaten
- 1 tsp vanilla extract
- 70 g/2½ oz white chocolate chips

Topping
100 g/3½ oz white chocolate, melted
2 tbsp dark chocolate sprinkles

Fairy Flyaway Cupcakes

1. Preheat the oven to 190°C/375°F/Gas Mark 5. Place 28 paper cases into bun tins or put double-layer paper cases onto baking trays.

2. Sift the flour and baking powder into a large bowl and add the butter, caster sugar, eggs and vanilla extract. Beat well until the mixture is smooth, then stir in enough of the milk to make a soft dropping consistency.

3. Divide the mixture between the paper cases. Bake in the preheated oven for 15–20 minutes, or until risen, firm and golden brown. Transfer the cupcakes to a wire rack to cool.

4. For the buttercream, beat together the butter, icing sugar and vanilla extract until smooth.

5. Use a serrated knife to cut a round from the top of each cupcake, then cut each round in half. Spread or pipe a little of the buttercream on top of each cake, then press the pieces of cake into it to resemble fairy wings. Decorate with the coloured sprinkles.

Makes 28

* 175 g/6 oz plain white flour
* 1 tbsp baking powder
* 175 g/6 oz unsalted butter, softened
* 175 g/6 oz golden caster sugar
* 3 eggs, beaten
* 1 tsp vanilla extract
  about 1 tbsp milk
  coloured sprinkles, to decorate

Buttercream
100 g/3½ oz unsalted butter, softened
200 g/7 oz icing sugar
½ tsp vanilla extract

47

Raspberry Ripple Cupcakes

1. Preheat the oven to 190°C/375°F/Gas Mark 5. Place 32 paper cases into bun tins or put double-layer paper cases onto baking trays.

2. Sift the flour, baking powder and cornflour into a large bowl and add the butter, caster sugar, eggs and almond extract. Beat well until the mixture is smooth. Mash the raspberries lightly with a fork, then fold into the mixture.

3. Divide the mixture between the paper cases. Bake in the preheated oven for 15–20 minutes, or until risen, firm and golden brown.

4. Transfer the cupcakes to a wire rack to cool. Sprinkle with vanilla sugar before serving.

Makes 32

- 175 g/6 oz plain white flour
- 1 tbsp baking powder
- 1 tbsp cornflour
- 175 g/6 oz unsalted butter, softened
- 175 g/6 oz caster sugar
- 3 eggs, beaten
- 1 tsp almond extract
- 200 g/7 oz fresh raspberries
- vanilla sugar, for sprinkling

48

Banana Passion Fruit Cupcakes

1. Preheat the oven to 190°C/375°F/Gas Mark 5. Place 30 paper cases into bun tins or put double-layer paper cases onto baking trays.

2. Sift the flour, baking powder and custard powder into a large bowl and add the butter, sugar, eggs and vanilla extract. Beat well until the mixture is smooth. Mash one of the bananas with 1 tablespoon of the lemon juice and stir into the mix.

3. Divide the mixture between the paper cases. Bake in the preheated oven for 15–20 minutes, or until risen, firm and golden brown. Transfer the cupcakes to a wire rack to cool.

4. Halve the passion fruit and scoop out the pulp into a small bowl, then stir in the honey. Thinly slice the remaining banana and brush with the remaining lemon juice. Place a banana slice on top of each cupcake and spread a little of the passion fruit glaze over the top.

Makes 30

* 175 g/6 oz plain white flour
* 1 tbsp baking powder
  1 tbsp custard powder
* 175 g/6 oz unsalted butter, softened
* 175 g/6 oz light muscovado sugar
* 3 eggs, beaten
* 1 tsp vanilla extract
  2 ripe bananas
* 2 tbsp lemon juice
  2 passion fruit
  2 tbsp clear honey

Christmas Cupcakes

1. Preheat the oven to 190°C/375°F/Gas Mark 5. Place 36 paper cases into bun tins or put double-layer paper cases onto baking trays.

2. Sift the flour, baking powder and cinnamon into a large bowl and add the butter, sugar, eggs and almond extract. Beat well until the mixture is smooth, then stir in the sherry, orange rind, ground almonds and mixed dried fruit.

3. Divide the mixture between the paper cases. Bake in the preheated oven for 15–20 minutes, or until risen, firm and golden brown. Transfer the cupcakes to a wire rack to cool.

4. To decorate, roll out about three quarters of the white icing fairly thinly and cut into 5-cm/2-inch rounds. Brush with a little water and fix one to the top of each cupcake.

5. Colour three quarters of the remaining icing green and colour the remainder red. Roll out the green icing and use a small cutter to cut into holly leaves, then shape tiny balls from the red icing to resemble berries.

6. Brush the leaves and berries with a little water, then attach on top of the cupcakes and leave to dry.

Makes 36

- 175 g/6 oz plain white flour
- 1 tbsp baking powder
- 1 tsp ground cinnamon
- 175 g/6 oz unsalted butter, softened
- 175 g/6 oz light muscovado sugar
- 3 eggs, beaten
- 1 tsp almond extract
- 2 tbsp medium sherry
- 1 tbsp finely grated orange rind
- 2 tbsp ground almonds
- 60 g/2¼ oz mixed dried fruit

To decorate
450 g/1 lb ready-to-roll soft white icing

a few drops of green and red edible food colouring

Blueberry Cupcakes with Soured Cream Frosting

① Preheat the oven to 190°C/375°F/Gas Mark 5. Place 30 paper cases into bun tins or put double-layer paper cases onto baking trays.

② Sift the flour and baking powder into a large bowl and add the butter, caster sugar, eggs and vanilla extract. Beat well until the mixture is smooth, then stir in the orange rind and 100g/3½ oz of the blueberries.

③ Divide the mixture between the paper cases. Bake in the preheated oven for 15–20 minutes, or until risen, firm and golden brown. Transfer the cupcakes to a wire rack to cool.

④ For the frosting, stir the soured cream into the icing sugar and mix well until smooth. Spoon a little frosting on top of each cupcake and top with the remaining blueberries. Leave to set.

Makes 30

* 175 g/6 oz plain white flour
* 1 tbsp baking powder
* 175 g/6 oz unsalted butter, softened
* 175 g/6 oz caster sugar
* 3 eggs, beaten
* 1 tsp vanilla extract
  finely grated rind of ½ orange
  150 g/5½ oz fresh blueberries

Frosting
3 tbsp soured cream
150 g/5½ oz icing sugar, sifted

51

Butterscotch Cupcakes

1. Preheat the oven to 190°C/375°F/Gas Mark 5. Place 28 paper cases into bun tins or put double-layer paper cases onto baking trays.

2. Sift the flour and baking powder into a large bowl and add the butter, sugar, eggs and vanilla extract. Beat well until the mixture is smooth.

3. Divide the mixture between the paper cases. Bake in the preheated oven for 15–20 minutes, or until risen, firm and golden brown. Transfer the cupcakes to a wire rack to cool.

4. For the topping, place the golden syrup, butter and sugar in a small pan and heat gently, stirring, until the sugar dissolves. Bring to the boil and cook, stirring, for about 1 minute. Drizzle over the cupcakes and leave to set.

Makes 28

- 175 g/6 oz plain white flour
- 1 tbsp baking powder
- 175 g/6 oz unsalted butter, softened
- 175 g/6 oz light muscovado sugar
- 3 eggs, beaten
- 1 tsp vanilla extract

Topping
2 tbsp golden syrup
25 g/1 oz unsalted butter
2 tbsp light muscovado sugar

Teatime Cupcakes

1. Preheat the oven to 180°C/350°F/Gas Mark 4. Place ten 200 ml/7 fl oz ovenproof teacups onto baking sheets.

2. Sift the flour, baking powder and mixed spice into a large bowl and add the butter, caster sugar, eggs and vanilla extract. Beat well until the mixture is smooth, then stir in the tea and half the currants.

3. Divide the mixture between the cups and sprinkle with the remaining currants. Bake in the preheated oven for 20–25 minutes, or until risen, firm and golden brown. Transfer the cupcakes to a wire rack to cool.

4. Dust the cupcakes with a little icing sugar and mixed spice before serving.

Makes 10

* 175 g/6 oz plain white flour
* 1 tbsp baking powder
* ½ tsp ground mixed spice
* 175 g/6 oz unsalted butter, softened
* 175 g/6 oz golden caster sugar
* 3 eggs, beaten
* 1 tsp vanilla extract
* 2 tbsp strong Earl Grey tea
* 55 g/2 oz currants
* icing sugar and mixed spice, for dusting

Jammy Cupcakes

1. Preheat the oven to 190°C/375°F/Gas Mark 5. Place 28 paper cases into bun tins or put double-layer paper cases onto baking trays.

2. Sift the flour, baking powder and custard powder into a large bowl and add the butter, caster sugar, eggs and vanilla extract. Beat well until the mixture is smooth.

3. Divide the mixture between the paper cases and place a half teaspoonful of jam onto the centre of each, without pressing down.

4. Bake in the preheated oven for 15–20 minutes, or until risen, firm and golden brown. Transfer the cupcakes to a wire rack to cool. Dust with icing sugar before serving.

Makes 28

* 175 g/6 oz plain white flour
* 1 tbsp baking powder
  1 tbsp custard powder
* 175 g/6 oz unsalted butter, softened
* 175 g/6 oz golden caster sugar
* 3 eggs, beaten
* 1 tsp vanilla extract
  70 g/2½ oz raspberry jam
  icing sugar, for dusting

54

Orange Saffron Mini Cupcakes

1. Preheat the oven to 190°C/375°F/Gas Mark 5. Arrange 90 mini paper cases on 2–3 baking sheets.

2. Heat 2 tablespoons of the orange juice with the saffron threads until almost boiling, then remove from the heat and leave to stand for 10 minutes.

3. Sift the flour and baking powder into a large bowl and add the butter, caster sugar and eggs. Beat well until the mixture is smooth, then stir in the orange rind and half the saffron and orange juice mixture.

4. Spoon the mixture into the paper cases. Bake in the preheated oven for 12–15 minutes, or until risen, firm and golden brown. Transfer the cupcakes to a wire rack to cool.

5. Mix the remaining saffron and orange juice mixture with the icing sugar to make a smooth paste, adding a little extra orange juice if needed. Spoon a little on top of each cupcake, decorate with strips of orange zest and leave to set.

Makes 90

※ 2–3 tbsp orange juice
pinch of saffron threads
※ 175 g/6 oz plain white flour
※ 1 tbsp baking powder
※ 175 g/6 oz unsalted butter, softened
※ 175 g/6 oz golden caster sugar
※ 3 eggs, beaten
finely grated rind of 1 orange
150 g/5½ oz icing sugar, sifted
fine strips of orange zest, to decorate

Chocolate Flake Cupcakes

1. Preheat the oven to 190°C/375°F/Gas Mark 5. Place 30 paper cases into bun tins or put double-layer paper cases onto baking trays.

2. Sift the flour and baking powder into a large bowl and add the butter, sugar, eggs and vanilla extract. Beat well until the mixture is smooth. Mix the milk with the cocoa powder and stir into the mixture.

3. Divide the mixture between the paper cases and sprinkle with about a quarter of the crumbled chocolate. Bake in the preheated oven for 15–20 minutes, or until risen, firm and golden brown. Transfer the cupcakes to a wire rack to cool.

4. When the cupcakes are cold, brush the tops with apricot jam and sprinkle with the remaining crumbled chocolate.

Makes 30

* 175 g/6 oz plain white flour
* 1 tbsp baking powder
* 175 g/6 oz unsalted butter, softened
* 175 g/6 oz golden caster sugar
* 3 eggs, beaten
* 1 tsp vanilla extract
* 2 tbsp milk
* 1 tbsp cocoa powder
* 70 g/2½ oz chocolate flake bars, crumbled
* 3 tbsp apricot jam, warmed

Chocolate Honeycomb Cupcakes

1. Preheat the oven to 190°C/375°F/Gas Mark 5. Place 30 paper cases into bun tins or put double-layer paper cases onto baking trays.

2. Sift the flour and baking powder into a large bowl and add the butter, caster sugar, eggs and vanilla extract. Beat well until the mixture is smooth, then stir in the chopped honeycomb.

3. Divide the mixture between the paper cases. Bake in the preheated oven for 15–20 minutes, or until risen, firm and golden brown. Transfer the cupcakes to a wire rack to cool.

4. For the topping, mix together the icing sugar, cocoa and water to make a smooth paste. Spoon a little on top of each cupcake and top with chunks of honeycomb. Leave to set.

Makes 30

* 175 g/6 oz plain white flour
* 1 tbsp baking powder
* 175 g/6 oz unsalted butter, softened
* 175 g/6 oz golden caster sugar
* 3 eggs, beaten
* 1 tsp vanilla extract
  40 g/1½ oz chocolate-covered honeycomb, finely chopped

Topping
200 g/7 oz icing sugar, sifted
2 tsp cocoa powder
about 2 tbsp water
40 g/1½ oz chocolate-covered honeycomb, cut into chunks

57

Coffee Fudge Cupcakes

1. Preheat the oven to 190°C/375°F/Gas Mark 5. Place 28 paper cases into bun tins or put double-layer paper cases onto baking trays.

2. Sift the flour and baking powder into a large bowl and add the butter, caster sugar, eggs and coffee extract. Beat well until the mixture is smooth, then beat in the milk.

3. Divide the mixture between the paper cases. Bake in the preheated oven for 15–20 minutes, or until risen, firm and golden brown. Transfer the cupcakes to a wire rack to cool.

4. For the frosting, place the butter, muscovado sugar, cream and coffee extract in a saucepan over a medium heat and stir until melted and smooth. Bring to the boil and boil, stirring, for 2 minutes. Remove from the heat and beat in the icing sugar.

5. Stir the frosting until smooth and thick, then spoon into a piping bag fitted with a large star nozzle. Pipe a swirl of frosting on top of each cupcake and top with a coffee bean.

Makes 28

* 175 g/6 oz plain white flour
* 1 tbsp baking powder
* 175 g/6 oz unsalted butter, softened
* 175 g/6 oz caster sugar
* 3 eggs, beaten
* 1 tsp coffee extract
* 2 tbsp milk

chocolate-covered coffee beans, to decorate

Frosting

55 g/2 oz unsalted butter

115 g/4 oz light muscovado sugar

2 tbsp single cream or milk

½ tsp coffee extract

400 g/14 oz icing sugar, sifted

Gingerbread Cupcakes

1. Preheat the oven to 190°C/375°F/Gas Mark 5. Place 30 paper cases into bun tins or put double-layer paper cases onto baking trays.

2. Sift the flour, baking powder, ginger and cinnamon into a large bowl and add the butter, muscovado sugar, eggs and vanilla extract. Beat well until the mixture is smooth.

3. Divide the mixture between the paper cases. Bake in the preheated oven for 15–20 minutes, or until risen, firm and golden brown. Transfer the cupcakes to a wire rack to cool.

4. For the frosting, beat together the butter, icing sugar and orange juice until smooth. Spoon a little frosting on top of each cupcake and top with the crystallized ginger.

Makes 30

- 175 g/6 oz plain white flour
- 1 tbsp baking powder
- 2 tsp ground ginger
- 1 tsp ground cinnamon
- 175 g/6 oz unsalted butter, softened
- 175 g/6 oz dark muscovado sugar
- 3 eggs, beaten
- 1 tsp vanilla extract

chopped crystallized ginger, to decorate

Frosting

85 g/3 oz unsalted butter, softened

150 g/5½ oz icing sugar, sifted

3 tbsp orange juice

Peppermint Chocolate Chip Cupcakes

1. Preheat the oven to 190°C/375°F/Gas Mark 5. Place 32 paper cases into bun tins or put double-layer paper cases onto baking trays.

2. Sift the flour and baking powder into a large bowl and add the butter, sugar, eggs and peppermint extract. Beat well until the mixture is smooth, then stir in half the chocolate chips.

3. Divide the mixture between the paper cases and sprinkle with the remaining chocolate chips. Bake in the preheated oven for 15–20 minutes, or until risen, firm and golden brown. Transfer the cupcakes to a wire rack to cool.

4. When cooled, drizzle the cupcakes with the melted chocolate and decorate with pieces of chocolate mint stick. Leave to set.

Makes 32

* 175 g/6 oz plain white flour
* 1 tbsp baking powder
* 175 g/6 oz unsalted butter, softened
* 175 g/6 oz caster sugar
* 3 eggs, beaten
* 1 tsp peppermint extract
* 70 g/2½ oz plain chocolate chips

Topping

100 g/3½ oz plain chocolate, melted

10 chocolate mint sticks, broken into short lengths

Marzipan Chunk Cupcakes

1. Preheat the oven to 190°C/375°F/Gas Mark 5. Place 32 paper cases into bun tins or put double-layer paper cases onto baking trays.

2. Sift the flour, cornflour and baking powder into a large bowl and add the butter, sugar, eggs and almond extract. Beat well until the mixture is smooth.

3. Divide the mixture between the paper cases and scatter a few pieces of marzipan on top of each. Bake in the preheated oven for 15–20 minutes, or until risen, firm and golden brown. Transfer the cupcakes to a wire rack to cool.

Makes 32

- 175 g/6 oz plain white flour
- 2 tsp cornflour
- 1 tbsp baking powder
- 175 g/6 oz unsalted butter, softened
- 175 g/6 oz caster sugar
- 3 eggs, beaten
- 1 tsp almond extract
- 85 g/3 oz golden marzipan, cut into 5-mm/¼-inch dice

Fruity

61

Raspberry & Pine Kernel Slices

1. Preheat the oven to 180°C/350°F/Gas Mark 4. Grease and line a 20 x 30-cm/8 x 12-inch rectangular cake tin.

2. Sift the flour and baking powder into a large bowl and add the butter, sugar, eggs and vanilla extract. Beat well until the mixture is smooth, then stir in the milk, raspberries and half the pine kernels.

3. Spoon the mixture into the prepared tin and smooth the surface with a palette knife. Scatter the remaining pine kernels over the surface. Bake in the preheated oven for 40–50 minutes, or until risen, firm and golden brown.

4. Leave to cool in the tin, then cut into slices when firm.

Makes 10

- oil or melted butter, for greasing
- 175 g/6 oz plain white flour
- 1 tbsp baking powder
- 175 g/6 oz unsalted butter, softened
- 175 g/6 oz caster sugar
- 3 eggs, beaten
- 1 tsp vanilla extract
- 2 tbsp milk
- 225 g/8 oz fresh raspberries
- 70 g/2½ oz pine kernels

62

Rhubarb & Ginger Cake

1. Preheat the oven to 180°C/350°F/Gas Mark 4. Grease and line a 23-cm/9-inch square deep cake tin.

2. Sift the flour and baking powder into a large bowl and add the butter, caster sugar, eggs and vanilla extract. Beat well until the mixture is smooth.

3. Spoon the mixture into the prepared tin and smooth the surface with a palette knife. Stir the cornflour into the rhubarb, then add the ginger and scatter evenly over the cake mixture.

4. Bake in the preheated oven for 50–60 minutes, or until risen, firm and golden brown. Leave to cool in the tin for about 10 minutes, then turn out and finish cooling on a wire rack.

5. For the icing, mix the icing sugar with the ginger syrup until smooth, then drizzle over the cake. Leave to set before cutting into slices.

Serves 8

* oil or melted butter, for greasing
* 175 g/6 oz plain white flour
* 2 tsp baking powder
* 175 g/6 oz unsalted butter, softened
* 175 g/6 oz caster sugar
* 3 eggs, beaten
* 1 tsp vanilla extract
* 1 tbsp cornflour
* 200 g/7 oz pink rhubarb, cut into 1-cm/½-inch slices
* 30 g/1 oz stem ginger, finely chopped

Icing
* 3 tbsp icing sugar
* 3 tsp stem ginger syrup (from the jar)

Pear & Hazelnut Streusel Cake

1. Preheat the oven to 180°C/350°F/Gas Mark 4. Grease and line a 23-cm/9-inch round spring-release cake tin.

2. For the streusel topping, mix the chopped hazelnuts, muscovado sugar, flour, cinnamon and melted butter in a small bowl with a fork to make a crumbly mixture.

3. Sift the flour and baking powder into a large bowl and add the butter, caster sugar, eggs and vanilla extract. Beat well until the mixture is smooth, then stir in the ground hazelnuts and half the chopped pears.

4. Spoon the mixture into the prepared tin and smooth the surface with a palette knife. Scatter over the remaining chopped pears and spread level. Sprinkle the streusel topping evenly over the cake.

5. Bake in the preheated oven for about 1 hour, or until risen, firm and golden brown. Leave to cool in the tin for 2–3 minutes, then remove the sides of the tin and finish cooling on a wire rack.

Serves 8

- oil or melted butter, for greasing
- 175 g/6 oz plain white flour
- 2 tsp baking powder
- 175 g/6 oz unsalted butter, softened
- 175 g/6 oz golden caster sugar
- 3 eggs, beaten
- 1 tsp vanilla extract
- 55 g/2 oz ground hazelnuts
- 2 firm ripe pears, peeled, cored and finely chopped

Streusel topping
- 50 g/1¾ oz toasted hazelnuts, finely chopped
- 40 g/1½ oz dark muscovado sugar
- 3 tbsp plain white flour
- ½ tsp ground cinnamon
- 25 g/1 oz unsalted butter, melted

Chewy Date & Sesame Slices

1. Preheat the oven to 180°C/350°F/Gas Mark 4. Grease and line a 30 x 23-cm/12 x 9-inch rectangular cake tin.

2. Place the dates and orange juice in a saucepan and heat, stirring occasionally, until boiling. Reduce the heat and simmer gently for about 5 minutes, until the liquid is absorbed. Remove from the heat and leave to cool.

3. Sift the flours and baking powder into a large bowl, adding any bran left in the sieve. Add the butter, sugar, eggs and vanilla extract. Beat well until the mixture is smooth, then stir in the soaked dates.

4. Spoon the mixture into the prepared tin and smooth the surface with a palette knife. Sprinkle the sesame seeds evenly over the top. Bake in the preheated oven for 25–30 minutes, or until risen, firm and golden brown.

5. Leave to cool in the tin, then cut into slices when firm.

Makes 12

- oil or melted butter, for greasing
- 200 g/7 oz pitted dates, roughly chopped
- 4 tbsp orange juice
- 85 g/3 oz plain white flour
- 85 g/3 oz plain wholemeal flour
- 1½ tsp baking powder
- 175 g/6 oz unsalted butter, softened
- 175 g/6 oz dark muscovado sugar
- 3 eggs, beaten
- 1 tsp vanilla extract
- 3 tbsp sesame seeds

65

Honeyed Apple Slices

1. Preheat the oven to 180°C/350°F/Gas Mark 4. Grease and line a 30 x 23-cm/12 x 9-inch rectangular cake tin.

2. Sift the flour, baking powder and allspice into a large bowl and add the butter, sugar, eggs and vanilla extract. Beat well until the mixture is smooth, then stir in the apple juice.

3. Spoon the mixture into the prepared tin and smooth the surface with a palette knife. Core and slice the apples and arrange them, overlapping, on top of the cake mixture, without pressing into the mix. Brush lightly with half the honey.

4. Bake in the preheated oven for 30–35 minutes, or until risen, firm and golden brown. Leave to cool in the tin for about 15 minutes, until firm, then cut into slices and finish cooling on a wire rack.

5. Brush with the remaining honey before serving.

Makes 12

* oil or melted butter, for greasing
* 175 g/6 oz plain white flour
* 2 tsp baking powder
* ½ tsp ground allspice
* 175 g/6 oz unsalted butter, softened
* 175 g/6 oz caster sugar
* 3 eggs, beaten
* 1 tsp vanilla extract
* 2 tbsp apple juice
* 4 red-skinned apples
* 3 tbsp clear honey, warmed

Banoffee Pecan Cake

1. Preheat the oven to 180°C/350°F/Gas Mark 4. Grease two 20-cm/8-inch sandwich cake tins and line the bases with baking paper.

2. Sift the flour and baking powder into a large bowl and add the butter, sugar, eggs and vanilla extract. Beat well until the mixture is smooth, then stir in the chopped pecans. Add the dulce de leche and stir to swirl through the mix.

3. Spoon the mixture into the prepared tins and smooth the surfaces with a palette knife. Bake in the preheated oven for 25–30 minutes, or until risen, firm and golden brown. Cool in the tins for 2–3 minutes, then turn out and finish cooling on a wire rack.

4. Reserve a few slices of banana for decoration and mash the remainder. Mix the mashed bananas with 3 tablespoons of the dulce de leche and use to sandwich the cakes together.

5. Whip the cream until thick, then swirl in the remaining dulce de leche. Spread over the cake and decorate with the reserved banana slices and the pecan halves.

Serves 6

* oil or melted butter, for greasing
* 175 g/6 oz plain white flour
* 1 tbsp baking powder
* 175 g/6 oz unsalted butter, softened
* 175 g/6 oz caster sugar
* 3 eggs, beaten
* 1 tsp vanilla extract
  40 g/1½ oz pecan nuts, finely chopped, plus extra pecan halves to decorate
  40 g/1½ oz dulce de leche

Filling and topping
2 bananas
5 tbsp dulce de leche
100 ml/3½ fl oz double cream

67

Tropical Fruit Ring

1. Preheat the oven to 160°C/325°F/Gas Mark 3. Grease a 1.5-litre/2¾-pint ring cake tin, preferably non-stick. Stir the lime juice into the dried tropical fruit and leave to soak for 15 minutes.

2. Sift the flour and baking powder into a large bowl and add the butter, caster sugar, eggs and vanilla extract. Beat well until the mixture is smooth, then stir in the soaked fruit.

3. Spoon the mixture into the prepared tin and smooth the surface with a palette knife. Bake in the preheated oven for 40–50 minutes, or until risen, firm and golden brown. Leave to cool in the tin for 10 minutes, then turn out and finish cooling on a wire rack.

4. For the icing, sift the icing sugar into a bowl, add the lime juice and stir until smooth. Spoon the icing over the cake and decorate with dried tropical fruit. Leave to set before slicing.

Serves 12

- oil or melted butter, for greasing
- 2 tbsp lime juice
- 100 g/3½ oz dried tropical fruit, such as mango, papaya and/or pineapple, finely chopped, plus extra to decorate
- 175 g/6 oz plain white flour
- 2½ tsp baking powder
- 175 g/6 oz unsalted butter, softened
- 175 g/6 oz golden caster sugar
- 3 eggs, beaten
- 1 tsp vanilla extract

Icing
70 g/2½ oz icing sugar
1 tbsp lime juice

68

Berry Crunch Cake

1. Preheat the oven to 180°C/350°F/Gas Mark 4. Grease a 23-cm/9-inch round spring-release cake tin and line the base with baking paper.

2. Sift the 175 g/6 oz flour and baking powder into a large bowl and add the butter, sugar, eggs and vanilla extract. Beat well until the mixture is smooth.

3. Spoon about half the mixture into the prepared tin and smooth the surface with a palette knife. Spread the berries evenly over the mixture. Stir the extra tablespoon of flour into the remaining mix. Spread out the crushed biscuits on a large plate. Using two spoons, toss small spoonfuls of the mix in the crushed biscuits, then arrange over the cake. Sprinkle over any remaining biscuit crumbs.

4. Bake in the preheated oven for 45–55 minutes, or until risen, firm and golden brown. Leave to cool in the tin for 2–3 minutes, then remove the sides and finish cooling on a wire rack. This cake is best eaten on the day of making.

Serves 8

- oil or melted butter, for greasing
- 175 g/6 oz plain white flour, plus 1 tbsp
- 2 tsp baking powder
- 175 g/6 oz unsalted butter, softened
- 175 g/6 oz caster sugar
- 3 eggs, beaten
- 1 tsp vanilla extract
- 225 g/8 oz fresh mixed berries, such as raspberries, blueberries and blackberries
- 70 g/2½ oz ginger nut biscuits, crushed

Mango & Ginger Roulade

1. Preheat the oven to 180°C/350°F/Gas Mark 4. Grease and line a 23 x 33-cm/9 x 13-inch Swiss roll tin with the paper 1 cm/½ inch above the rim. Lay a sheet of baking paper on the work surface and sprinkle with caster sugar.

2. Sift the flour and baking powder into a large bowl and add the butter, sugar, eggs and vanilla extract. Beat well until the mixture is smooth, then beat in the orange juice.

3. Spoon the mixture into the prepared tin and smooth into the corners with a palette knife. Bake in the preheated oven for 15–20 minutes, or until risen, firm and golden brown.

4. Meanwhile, peel and stone the mango. Reserve a few pieces for decoration and finely chop the remainder. Transfer the chopped mango to a small bowl and stir in 2 tablespoons of the glacé ginger.

5. When cooked, turn the sponge out onto the sugared baking paper and spread with the mango mixture. Roll up the sponge firmly from one short side to enclose the filling, keeping the paper around the outside to hold it in place. Lift onto a wire rack to cool, removing the paper when firm.

6. When cold, top with spoonfuls of crème fraîche and decorate with the reserved mango and the remaining glacé ginger.

Serves 6

- oil or melted butter, for greasing
- 150 g/5½ oz plain white flour
- 1½ tsp baking powder
- 175 g/6 oz unsalted butter, softened
- 175 g/6 oz golden caster sugar, plus extra for sprinkling
- 3 eggs, beaten
- 1 tsp vanilla extract
- 2 tbsp orange juice
- 1 large ripe mango
- 3 tbsp chopped glacé ginger
- 5 tbsp crème fraîche

70

Banana & Carrot Squares

1. Preheat the oven to 160°C/325°F/Gas Mark 3. Grease and line a 23-cm/9-inch square cake tin.

2. Sift the flour, baking powder and nutmeg into a bowl and add the butter, caster sugar and eggs. Beat well until smooth, then stir in the lemon juice, banana, carrots and walnuts.

3. Spoon the mixture into the prepared tin and smooth the surface with a palette knife. Bake in the preheated oven for 45–55 minutes, or until risen, firm and golden brown.

4. Leave to cool in the tin for 5 minutes, then turn out onto a wire rack to finish cooling. Cut into squares when cold.

5. For the frosting, mix the ricotta with the icing sugar and lemon rind in a small bowl. Pipe or spoon a little frosting on top of each square of cake, top with a banana chip and sprinkle with nutmeg.

Makes 16

* oil or melted butter, for greasing
* 175 g/6 oz plain white flour
* 1 tbsp baking powder
* 1 tsp ground nutmeg
* 175 g/6 oz unsalted butter, softened
* 175 g/6 oz golden caster sugar
* 3 eggs, beaten
* 1 tbsp lemon juice
* 1 banana, mashed
* 140 g/5 oz carrots, coarsely grated
* 40 g/1½ oz walnuts, finely chopped
* dried banana chips and freshly grated nutmeg, to decorate

Frosting
250 g/9 oz ricotta cheese
70 g/2½ oz icing sugar
finely grated rind of ½ lemon

71

Peachy Oat Crumble Cake

1. Preheat the oven to 180°C/350°F/Gas Mark 4. Grease a 25-cm/10-inch round spring-release cake tin and line the base with baking paper.

2. Sift the flour, baking powder and star anise into a large bowl and add the butter, sugar, eggs and vanilla extract. Beat well until the mixture is smooth.

3. Spoon the mixture into the prepared tin and smooth the surface with a palette knife. Arrange the chopped peaches evenly over the top.

4. For the topping, mix together the oats and sugar in a small bowl, then stir in the melted butter to make a crumbly mix. Spread evenly over the peaches.

5. Bake in the preheated oven for about 1 hour, or until risen, firm and golden brown. Leave to cool in the tin for 2–3 minutes, then remove the sides and finish cooling on a wire rack. This cake is best eaten on the day of making.

Serves 8–10

- oil or melted butter, for greasing
- 175 g/6 oz plain white flour
- 1 tbsp baking powder
- 1 tsp ground star anise
- 175 g/6 oz unsalted butter, softened
- 175 g/6 oz golden caster sugar
- 3 eggs, beaten
- 1 tsp vanilla extract
- 4 ripe peaches, stoned and roughly chopped

Topping
125 g/4½ oz porridge oats
55 g/2 oz golden caster sugar
55 g/2 oz unsalted butter, melted

Chunky Orange & Peanut Squares

1. Preheat the oven to 160°C/325°F/Gas Mark 3. Grease and line a 23-cm/9-inch square cake tin.

2. Finely grate the rind from the orange and reserve. Use a sharp knife to cut off all the peel and white pith, then cut the flesh into small chunks.

3. Sift the flour and baking powder into a large bowl and add the butter, peanut butter, caster sugar, eggs and vanilla extract. Beat well until the mixture is smooth, then stir in the orange rind and orange chunks.

4. Spoon the mixture into the prepared tin and smooth the surface with a palette knife. Bake in the preheated oven for 40–50 minutes, or until risen, firm and golden brown. Leave to cool in the tin for about 10 minutes, then turn out and finish cooling on a wire rack.

5. For the icing, mix together the peanut butter, orange juice and icing sugar, then spread over the cooled cake. Cut into squares before serving.

Makes 9

* oil or melted butter, for greasing
* 1 orange
* 175 g/6 oz plain white flour
* 1½ tsp baking powder
* 100 g/3½ oz unsalted butter, softened
* 70 g/3 oz crunchy peanut butter
* 175 g/6 oz caster sugar
* 3 eggs, beaten
* 1 tsp vanilla extract

Icing
* 55 g/2 oz crunchy peanut butter
* 2 tbsp orange juice
* 55 g/2 oz icing sugar

Seeded Pear Bars

1. Preheat the oven to 180°C/350°F/Gas Mark 4. Grease and line a 30 x 23-cm/12 x 9-inch rectangular cake tin.

2. Cut the pears into quarters, remove the core and cut each quarter into 3–4 long slices. Brush with half the lemon juice.

3. Sift the flour and baking powder into a large bowl and add the butter, muscovado sugar, eggs and vanilla extract. Beat well until the mixture is smooth, then stir in the remaining lemon juice, the lemon rind, oats, and sunflower and pumpkin seeds.

4. Spoon the mixture into the prepared tin and smooth the surface with a palette knife. Arrange the pear slices overlapping on top, without pressing into the mixture, and sprinkle with the demerara sugar.

5. Bake in the preheated oven for 35–40 minutes, or until risen, firm and golden brown. Leave to cool in the tin for about 15 minutes, until firm, then cut into bars and finish cooling on a wire rack.

Makes 14

- oil or melted butter, for greasing
- 3 firm ripe pears
- 2 tbsp lemon juice
- 175 g/6 oz plain white flour
- 2 tsp baking powder
- 175 g/6 oz unsalted butter, softened
- 175 g/6 oz light muscovado sugar
- 3 eggs, beaten
- 1 tsp vanilla extract
- finely grated rind of 1 lemon
- 55 g/2 oz porridge oats
- 25 g/1 oz sunflower seeds
- 25 g/1 oz pumpkin seeds
- 1 tbsp demerara sugar

74

Strawberry Sponge Slices

1. Preheat the oven to 180°C/350°F/Gas Mark 4. Grease and line a 23 x 33-cm/9 x 13-inch Swiss roll tin with the paper 1 cm/½ inch above the rim.

2. Sift the flour and baking powder into a large bowl and add the butter, sugar, eggs and vanilla extract. Beat well until the mixture is smooth, then beat in the milk.

3. Spoon the mixture into the prepared tin and smooth into the corners with a palette knife. Bake in the preheated oven for 15–20 minutes, or until risen, firm and golden brown. Leave to cool in the tin.

4. When the cake is cold, cut crossways into three rectangles. Hull and chop the strawberries, reserving 4–5 whole for decoration. Stir the chopped strawberries into the mascarpone and use to sandwich together the cakes.

5. To serve, dust the cake with icing sugar. Hull and slice the reserved strawberries and arrange on top.

Makes 6–8

- oil or melted butter, for greasing
- 150 g/5½ oz plain white flour
- 1½ tsp baking powder
- 175 g/6 oz unsalted butter, softened
- 175 g/6 oz caster sugar
- 3 eggs, beaten
- 1 tsp vanilla extract
- 2 tbsp milk
- 250 g/9 oz fresh strawberries
- 250 g/9 oz mascarpone cheese
- icing sugar, for dusting

Blueberry Orange Streusel Cake

1. Preheat the oven to 160°C/325°F/Gas Mark 3. Grease a 23-cm/9-inch round spring-release cake tin and line the base with baking paper.

2. For the topping, place all the ingredients in a bowl and mix with a fork to make a crumbly mixture.

3. Sift the flour and baking powder into a large bowl and add the butter, sugar, eggs and vanilla extract. Beat well until the mixture is smooth, then add the orange rind, ground almonds and half the blueberries.

4. Spoon the mixture into the prepared tin, smooth the surface with a palette knife and scatter over the remaining blueberries. Spread the crumble topping evenly over the top, covering completely.

5. Bake in the preheated oven for 1 hour–1 hour 10 minutes, or until risen, firm and golden brown. Leave to cool in the tin for 10 minutes, then remove the sides of the tin and finish cooling on a wire rack.

Serves 8–10

* oil or melted butter, for greasing
* 175 g/6 oz plain white flour
  2 tsp baking powder
* 175 g/6 oz unsalted butter, softened
* 175 g/6 oz caster sugar
* 3 eggs, beaten
* 1 tsp vanilla extract
  finely grated rind of ½ orange
  55 g/2 oz ground almonds
  125 g/4½ oz fresh blueberries

Topping
55 g/2 oz plain white flour
25 g/1 oz unsalted butter, softened
25 g/1 oz caster sugar
finely grated rind of ½ orange

Kiwi Fruit Cake with Lemon Frosting

1. Preheat the oven to 160°C/325°F/Gas Mark 3. Grease and line a 1.2-litre/2-pint loaf tin.

2. Sift the flour and baking powder into a large bowl and add the butter, caster sugar, eggs and vanilla extract. Beat well until the mixture is smooth, then stir in half the chopped kiwi fruit.

3. Spoon the mixture into the prepared tin and smooth the surface with a palette knife. Scatter over the remaining chopped kiwi fruit. Bake in the preheated oven for about 1 hour, or until risen, firm and golden brown.

4. Leave to cool in the tin for 10 minutes, then turn out and finish cooling on a wire rack.

5. For the frosting, beat together the cream cheese, lemon rind and icing sugar until smooth. Spread the frosting over the cake and top with kiwi fruit slices.

Serves 8

* oil or melted butter, for greasing
* 175 g/6 oz plain white flour
  2 tsp baking powder
* 175 g/6 oz unsalted butter, softened
* 175 g/6 oz caster sugar
* 3 eggs, beaten
* 1 tsp vanilla extract
  2 kiwi fruit, peeled and chopped into 1-cm/½-inch dice, plus extra slices to decorate

Frosting
55 g/2 oz cream cheese
1 tbsp grated lemon rind
115 g/4 oz icing sugar

77

Chunky Apricot Loaf

1. Preheat the oven to 160°C/325°F/Gas Mark 3. Grease and line a 1.2-litre/2-pint loaf tin.

2. Sift the flour and baking powder into a large bowl and add the butter, sugar, eggs and almond extract. Beat well until the mixture is smooth, then stir in the orange juice and 150 g/5½ oz of the dried apricots.

3. Spoon the mixture into the prepared tin and smooth the surface with a palette knife. Sprinkle with the remaining dried apricots. Bake in the preheated oven for about 1 hour, or until risen, firm and golden brown.

4. Leave to cool in the tin for 10 minutes, then turn out and finish cooling on a wire rack.

5. Warm the apricot jam in a saucepan with the lemon juice and brush lightly over the cake top. Cut into slices to serve.

Serves 8

- oil or melted butter, for greasing
- 250 g/9 oz plain white flour
- 2 tsp baking powder
- 175 g/6 oz unsalted butter, softened
- 175 g/6 oz golden caster sugar
- 3 eggs, beaten
- 1 tsp almond extract
- 2 tbsp orange juice
- 200 g/7 oz ready-to-eat dried apricots, chopped
- 3 tbsp apricot jam
- 1 tbsp lemon juice

Cranberry Coconut Ring

1. Preheat the oven to 180°C/350°F/Gas Mark 4. Grease a 1.5-litre/2¾-pint ring cake tin, preferably non-stick.

2. Sift the flour and baking powder into a large bowl and add the butter, sugar, eggs and vanilla extract. Beat well until the mixture is smooth, then stir in the cranberries, cranberry juice and desiccated coconut.

3. Spoon the mixture into the prepared tin and smooth the surface with a palette knife. Bake in the preheated oven for 30–35 minutes, or until risen, firm and golden brown.

4. Leave to cool in the tin for 5 minutes, then turn out and finish cooling on a wire rack. Spoon the cranberry sauce on top of the cake, then sprinkle with coconut shreds and serve.

Serves 10

* oil or melted butter, for greasing
* 175 g/6 oz plain white flour
* 1 tbsp baking powder
* 175 g/6 oz unsalted butter, softened
* 175 g/6 oz caster sugar
* 3 eggs, beaten
* 1 tsp vanilla extract
  70 g/2½ oz dried cranberries
* 2 tbsp cranberry juice
  55 g/2 oz desiccated coconut
  3 tbsp cranberry sauce
  2 tbsp toasted long-shred coconut

Pineapple Hummingbird Cake

1. Preheat the oven to 180°C/350°F/Gas Mark 4. Grease three 23-cm/9-inch sandwich cake tins and line the bases with baking paper.

2. Sift the flour, baking powder and cinnamon into a bowl and add the caster sugar, oil, eggs and vanilla extract. Beat well until the mixture is smooth, then stir in the chopped pecans, banana and crushed pineapple.

3. Divide the mixture between the prepared tins, spreading evenly. Bake in the preheated oven for 20–25 minutes, or until risen, firm and golden brown.

4. Leave to cool in the tins for 2–3 minutes, then turn out onto a wire rack to finish cooling.

5. For the frosting, beat together the soft cheese, butter, vanilla extract and icing sugar until smooth. Sandwich the cakes together with about two thirds of the frosting. Spread the remaining frosting on top, then decorate with pineapple pieces and pecan nuts.

Serves 8–10

- oil or melted butter, for greasing
- 175 g/6 oz plain white flour
- 1 tbsp baking powder
- 1 tsp ground cinnamon
- 175 g/6 oz caster sugar
- 175 ml/6 fl oz sunflower oil
- 3 eggs, beaten
- 1 tsp vanilla extract
- 55 g/2 oz pecan nuts, finely chopped
- 2 small ripe bananas, mashed
- 85 g/3 oz canned crushed pineapple, drained
- pineapple pieces and pecan nuts, to decorate

Frosting
- 175 g/6 oz full-fat soft cheese
- 55 g/2 oz unsalted butter, softened
- 1 tsp vanilla extract
- 400 g/14 oz icing sugar, sifted

80

Chocolate & Cherry Gateau

1. Preheat the oven to 180°C/350°F/Gas Mark 4. Grease two 20-cm/8-inch sandwich cake tins and line the bases with baking paper.

2. Sift the flour, cocoa and baking powder into a large bowl and add the butter, caster sugar, eggs and vanilla extract. Beat well until the mixture is smooth, then stir in the milk.

3. Divide the mixture between the prepared tins and smooth the tops with a palette knife. Bake in the preheated oven for 25–30 minutes, or until risen and firm to the touch. Leave to cool in the tins for 2–3 minutes, then turn out and finish cooling on wire racks.

4. When the cakes are cold, sprinkle with the kirsch, if using. Whip the cream with the icing sugar until thick, then spread about a third over the top of one of the cakes. Spread the cherries over the cream and place the second cake on top.

5. Spread the remaining cream over the top and sides of the cake and decorate with grated chocolate and fresh whole cherries.

Serves 8

* oil or melted butter, for greasing
  150 g/5½ oz plain white flour
  2 tbsp cocoa powder
* 1 tbsp baking powder
* 175 g/6 oz unsalted butter, softened
* 175 g/6 oz golden caster sugar
* 3 eggs, beaten
* 1 tsp vanilla extract
* 2 tbsp milk
  3 tbsp kirsch or brandy (optional)
  grated chocolate and fresh whole cherries, to decorate

Filling and topping
450 ml/16 fl oz double or whipping cream
2 tbsp icing sugar
225 g/8 oz fresh dark red cherries, stoned

Warming

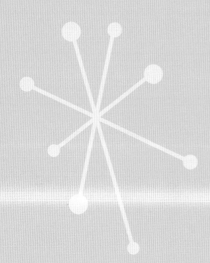

81

Plum Sponge Cake

1. Preheat the oven to 160°C/325°F/Gas Mark 3. Grease and line a 32 x 23-cm/13 x 9-inch rectangular cake tin.

2. Sift the flour and baking powder into a large bowl and add the butter, sugar, eggs and almond extract. Beat well until the mixture is smooth, then stir in the ground almonds.

3. Spoon the mixture into the prepared tin and smooth the surface with a palette knife. Arrange the plum quarters, skin-side down, over the mixture, without pressing them in, then scatter over the flaked almonds and demerara sugar.

4. Bake in the preheated oven for 50–60 minutes, or until risen, firm and golden brown. Cut into squares and serve warm with cream or yogurt.

Serves 6

* oil or melted butter, for greasing
* 175 g/6 oz plain white flour
  2 tsp baking powder
* 175 g/6 oz unsalted butter, softened
* 175 g/6 oz golden caster sugar
* 3 eggs, beaten
* 1 tsp almond extract
  70 g/2½ oz ground almonds
  8–10 large red plums, quartered and stoned
  3 tbsp flaked almonds
  2 tbsp demerara sugar
  cream or yogurt, to serve

82

Mango & Coconut Brûlée Cake

1. Preheat the oven to 180°C/350°F/Gas Mark 4. Grease a 23-cm/9-inch round deep cake tin and line the base with baking paper.

2. Arrange the mango evenly over the base of the prepared tin. Sift the flour and baking powder into a large bowl and add the butter, caster sugar and eggs. Beat well until the mixture is smooth, then stir in the lime juice, lime rind and desiccated coconut.

3. Spoon the mixture over the mango and smooth the surface with a palette knife. Bake in the preheated oven for 40–50 minutes, or until risen, firm and golden brown.

4. Leave to cool in the tin for 2–3 minutes, then turn out onto a flameproof dish. Preheat the grill to high. Sprinkle the top of the cake with granulated sugar and place under the hot grill for 2–3 minutes, until browned. Alternatively, use a chef's blowtorch to brown the top.

5. Serve hot, sprinkled with coconut shreds and cut into slices.

Serves 6

- oil or melted butter, for greasing
- 1 large ripe mango, diced
- 175 g/6 oz plain white flour
- 1 tbsp baking powder
- 175 g/6 oz unsalted butter, softened
- 175 g/6 oz caster sugar
- 3 eggs, beaten
- 2 tbsp lime juice
- finely grated rind of 1 lime
- 30 g/1 oz desiccated coconut
- 2 tbsp granulated sugar
- toasted long-shred coconut, to decorate

Toffee Apple Upside-down Cake

1. Preheat the oven to 180°C/350°F/Gas Mark 4. Grease a 23-cm/9-inch round deep cake tin with a solid base.

2. For the toffee apple topping, place the butter and sugar in a heavy-based saucepan with the water and heat gently until melted, then bring to the boil. Reduce the heat and cook, stirring, until it turns to a deep golden caramel colour. Pour quickly into the cake tin, tilting to cover the base evenly.

3. Peel, core and thickly slice the apples, toss with the lemon juice and spread evenly over the base of the cake tin.

4. Sift the flour and baking powder into a large bowl and add the butter, sugar, eggs and vanilla extract. Beat well until the mixture is smooth, then stir in the lemon rind.

5. Spoon the mixture over the apples and smooth the surface with a palette knife. Bake in the preheated oven for 40–50 minutes, or until risen and golden brown.

6. Leave to cool in the tin for 2–3 minutes, then turn out carefully onto a warmed serving plate. Serve with cream.

Serves 6

- oil or melted butter, for greasing
- 175 g/6 oz plain white flour
- 1 tbsp baking powder
- 175 g/6 oz unsalted butter, softened
- 175 g/6 oz golden caster sugar
- 3 eggs, beaten
- 1 tsp vanilla extract
- finely grated rind of 1 lemon
- cream, to serve

Toffee apple topping
- 55 g/2 oz unsalted butter
- 100 g/3½ oz caster sugar
- 1 tbsp water
- 4 eating apples
- 2 tbsp lemon juice

Mocha Puddings

1. Preheat the oven to 200°C/400°F/Gas Mark 6. Grease and line six 200-ml/7-fl oz individual metal pudding basins.

2. Sift the flour, cocoa and baking powder into a large bowl and add the butter, sugar, eggs and coffee extract. Beat well until the mixture is smooth.

3. Spoon the mixture into the prepared pudding basins. Place a square of chocolate on top of each. Bake in the preheated oven for 20–25 minutes, or until risen and firm to the touch.

4. For the sauce, place the cream, chocolate and coffee extract in a small saucepan and heat gently without boiling, stirring, until melted and smooth. Turn out the puddings and serve with the sauce poured over them.

Makes 6

* oil or melted butter, for greasing
* 175 g/6 oz plain white flour
* 2 tbsp cocoa powder
* 2 tsp baking powder
* 175 g/6 oz unsalted butter, softened
* 175 g/6 oz light muscovado sugar
* 3 eggs, beaten
* 1 tsp coffee extract
* 6 small squares plain chocolate

Sauce

250 ml/9 fl oz single cream

100 g/3½ oz plain chocolate, broken into pieces

1 tsp coffee extract

85

Lemon Surprise Cakes

1. Preheat the oven to 180°C/350°F/Gas Mark 4. Grease six 200-ml/7-fl oz ovenproof teacups or ramekins and place in a roasting tin.

2. Sift the flour and baking powder into a large bowl and add the butter, sugar and egg yolks. Beat well until the mixture is smooth, then stir in the lemon rind, lemon juice and milk. In a separate bowl, whisk the egg whites until they hold stiff peaks. Fold into the creamed mixture.

3. Spoon the mixture into the prepared teacups. Pour enough hot water into the tin to come halfway up the sides of the teacups. Bake in the preheated oven for 30–35 minutes, or until risen, firm and golden brown.

4. Transfer the teacups to warmed serving plates. There should be a light custard layer under the sponge.

Makes 6

* oil or melted butter, for greasing
* 175 g/6 oz plain white flour
* 1 tbsp baking powder
* 175 g/6 oz unsalted butter, softened
* 175 g/6 oz caster sugar
* 3 eggs, separated
  finely grated rind and juice of 2 lemons
  150 ml/5 fl oz milk

Peach & Cinnamon Cobbler

1. Preheat the oven to 160°C/325°F/Gas Mark 3. Grease a 23-cm/9-inch round spring-release cake tin and line the base with baking paper.

2. Sift the flour, baking powder and cinnamon into a large bowl and add the butter, sugar, eggs and vanilla extract. Beat well until the mixture is smooth.

3. Spoon half the mixture into the prepared tin and smooth the surface with a palette knife. Arrange the peaches on top. Stir the cornflakes lightly into the remaining mixture, then drop spoonfuls of the mix over the peaches.

4. Bake in the preheated oven for about 1 hour, or until risen, firm and golden brown. Serve hot with whipped cream.

Serves 6

* oil or melted butter, for greasing
* 175 g/6 oz plain white flour
  2 tsp baking powder
  1 tsp ground cinnamon
* 175 g/6 oz unsalted butter, softened
* 175 g/6 oz golden caster sugar
* 3 eggs, beaten
* 1 tsp vanilla extract
  3 ripe peaches or nectarines, stoned and roughly chopped
  70 g/2½ oz cornflakes, lightly crushed
  lightly whipped cream, to serve

Whole Orange & Almond Cake

1. Preheat the oven to 160°C/325°F/Gas Mark 3. Grease and line a 23-cm/9-inch round deep cake tin.

2. Wash the oranges and place in a saucepan, then cover with boiling water and simmer for 1 hour, covered, until soft. Drain and leave to cool slightly, then cut the oranges in half and remove and discard any pips. Purée in a food processor or blender until smooth, then stir in the ground almonds.

3. Sift the flour and baking powder into a large bowl and add the butter, sugar, eggs and orange flower water. Beat well until the mixture is smooth. Add the orange and almond mixture and the orange juice, mixing evenly.

4. Spoon the mixture into the prepared tin and smooth the surface with a palette knife. Bake in the preheated oven for 40–50 minutes, or until firm and golden brown.

5. Leave to cool in the tin for 2–3 minutes, then turn out and serve warm, topped with the flaked almonds and strips of orange zest.

Serves 8–10

* oil or melted butter, for greasing
* 2 oranges
* 55 g/2 oz ground almonds
* 115 g/4 oz plain white flour
* 1 tbsp baking powder
* 85 g/3 oz unsalted butter, softened
* 175 g/6 oz golden caster sugar
* 3 eggs, beaten
* 1 tsp orange flower water
* 2 tbsp orange juice
* 2 tbsp toasted flaked almonds
* strips of orange zest, to decorate

Lime Halva Cake

1. Preheat the oven to 180°C/350°F/Gas Mark 4. Grease and line a 20-cm/8-inch square deep cake tin.

2. Sift the semolina and baking powder into a large bowl and add the butter, sugar and eggs. Beat well until the mixture is smooth, stir in the ground almonds, lime rind and juice.

3. Spoon the mixture into the prepared tin and smooth the surface with a palette knife. Bake in the preheated oven for 30–35 minutes, or until risen and golden brown.

4. Meanwhile, to make the syrup, place the lime juice, sugar, water and cinnamon stick in a pan and heat gently, stirring, until the sugar dissolves. Add the lime slices and simmer for 1–2 minutes, then remove carefully and set aside. Bring the syrup to the boil and boil for 6–8 minutes, until syrupy and reduced by half. Discard the cinnamon stick.

5. Turn out the halva cake and arrange the lime slices over the top. Spoon over the lime syrup evenly and serve warm.

Serves 9

oil or melted butter, for greasing
250 g/9 oz semolina
1 tbsp baking powder
175 g/6 oz unsalted butter, softened
175 g/6 oz golden caster sugar
3 eggs, beaten
100 g/3½ oz ground almonds
finely grated rind and juice of 1 lime

Syrup
juice of 2 limes
175 g/6 oz caster sugar
200 ml/7 fl oz water
1 cinnamon stick
1 lime, thinly sliced

Apple Cider Cake

1. Preheat the oven to 160°C/325°F/Gas Mark 3. Grease a 2-litre/3½-pint ovenproof dish, about 5.5 cm/2¼ inches deep.

2. Cut a fairly thick slice from the stalk end of the apples and reserve. Remove the core from the apples then replace the tops.

3. Sift the flour and baking powder into a large bowl and add the butter, caster sugar, eggs and vanilla extract. Beat well until the mixture is smooth, then beat in the cider.

4. Spoon the mixture into the prepared dish and smooth the surface with a palette knife. Press the apples into the mixture then brush with butter. Mix the cinnamon into the demerara sugar and sprinkle over the apples.

5. Bake in the preheated oven for 1–1¼ hours, or until risen, firm and golden brown. Serve warm with cream or yogurt.

Serves 6

- ✳ melted butter, for greasing and brushing
- 6 small apples
- ✳ 175 g/6 oz plain white flour
- 2 tsp baking powder
- ✳ 175 g/6 oz unsalted butter, softened
- ✳ 175 g/6 oz golden caster sugar
- ✳ 3 eggs, beaten
- ✳ 1 tsp vanilla extract
- 2 tbsp dry cider
- ¼ tsp ground cinnamon
- 1 tbsp demerara sugar
- cream or yogurt, to serve

Apple & Blackberry Sponge

1. Preheat the oven to 160°C/325°F/Gas Mark 3. Grease a 1.5-litre/2¾-pint ovenproof pudding basin.

2. Peel and core the apple and cut half into dice, then mix with the blackberries and demerara sugar. Spoon into the base of the prepared basin. Coarsely grate the remaining apple.

3. Sift the flour and baking powder into a bowl and add the butter, sugar, eggs and vanilla extract. Beat well until smooth, then stir in the grated apple.

4. Spoon the mixture into the basin and spread the top level. Bake for 1 hour–1 hour 10 minutes, or until risen, firm and golden brown.

5. Leave to cool in the basin for 2 minutes, then turn out onto a warmed serving plate. Serve with cream.

Serves 6–8

* oil or melted butter, for greasing
* 1 cooking apple
* 115 g/4 oz fresh blackberries
* 2 tbsp demerara sugar
* 175 g/6 oz plain white flour
* 2 tsp baking powder
* 175 g/6 oz unsalted butter, softened
* 175 g/6 oz caster sugar
* 3 eggs, beaten
* 1 tsp vanilla extract
* cream, to serve

91

Individual Sultana Syrup Sponges

1. Preheat the oven to 160°C/325°F/Gas Mark 3. Grease a 12-hole muffin tin and place a teaspoonful of the golden syrup into the base of each hole.

2. Sift the flours, baking powder and allspice into a large bowl, adding any bran left in the sieve, then add the butter, sugar, eggs and vanilla extract. Beat well until the mixture is smooth, then stir in half the sultanas.

3. Divide the mixture between the prepared holes in the muffin tin and scatter the remaining sultanas on top. Bake in the preheated oven for 20–25 minutes, or until risen, firm and golden brown.

4. Leave to stand for 2 minutes, then turn out onto warmed serving plates. Serve with cream.

Makes 12

- oil or melted butter, for greasing
- 4 tbsp golden syrup
- 125 g/4½ oz plain white flour
- 55 g/2 oz plain wholemeal flour
- 1 tbsp baking powder
- 1 tsp ground allspice
- 175 g/6 oz unsalted butter, softened
- 175 g/6 oz golden caster sugar
- 3 eggs, beaten
- 1 tsp vanilla extract
- 55 g/2 oz sultanas
- cream, to serve

Cherry Puff Pudding

1. Preheat the oven to 180°C/350°F/Gas Mark 4. Grease a 2-litre/3½-pint ovenproof dish, about 5.5 cm/2¼ inches deep.

2. Sift the 175 g/6 oz flour with the baking powder, then add the butter, caster sugar, eggs and almond extract. Beat well until the mixture is smooth. Stir the 2 tablespoons of flour into the cherries, then stir half the cherries into the mix.

3. In a separate bowl, whisk the egg whites until they hold soft peaks. Fold the whites into the mixture using a large metal spoon.

4. Spoon the mixture into the prepared dish and scatter over the remaining cherries. Bake in the preheated oven for 45–55 minutes, or until risen and golden brown.

5. Scatter the flaked almonds over the pudding, then dust with icing sugar and serve immediately.

Serves 6–8

- oil or melted butter, for greasing
- 175 g/6 oz plain white flour, plus 2 tbsp extra
- 1 tbsp baking powder
- 175 g/6 oz unsalted butter, softened
- 175 g/6 oz caster sugar
- 3 eggs, beaten
- 1 tsp almond extract
- 300 g/10½ oz stoned fresh cherries
- 2 egg whites
- 1 tbsp flaked almonds, toasted
- icing sugar, for dusting

Syrup Apricot Ring

1. Preheat the oven to 180°C/350°F/Gas Mark 4. Brush a 23-cm/9-inch Bundt cake tin generously with melted butter.

2. Spoon the golden syrup over the base of the prepared tin, tilting to cover the base evenly. Arrange about 20 apricots in the golden syrup to cover the base of the tin. Finely chop the remaining apricots and place in a small pan with the orange juice. Bring to the boil, then remove from the heat and leave to stand to absorb the liquid.

3. Sift the flour and baking powder into a large bowl and add the butter, sugar, eggs and vanilla extract. Beat well until the mixture is smooth, then stir in the lemon rind and the soaked apricots.

4. Spoon the mixture into the tin and smooth the surface with a palette knife. Bake in the preheated oven for 35–40 minutes, or until risen, firm and golden brown.

5. Leave to cool in the tin for 2–3 minutes, then turn out carefully onto a warmed serving plate. Serve with a little extra golden syrup for drizzling over the top.

Serves 8

- melted butter, for greasing
- 3 tbsp golden syrup, plus extra to serve
- 175 g/6 oz ready-to-eat dried apricots
- 2 tbsp orange juice
- 175 g/6 oz plain white flour
- 2 tsp baking powder
- 175 g/6 oz unsalted butter, softened
- 175 g/6 oz light muscovado sugar
- 3 eggs, beaten
- 1 tsp vanilla extract
- finely grated rind of 1 lemon

94

Gooey Orange Chocolate Chip Cake

1. Preheat the oven to 180°C/350°F/Gas Mark 4. Grease and line a 23-cm/9-inch square cake tin.

2. Finely grate the rind from one of the oranges and reserve. Use a sharp knife to cut off all the peel and white pith from both oranges and carefully remove the segments, reserving any spare juices to add to the sauce. Chop half the segments into small pieces.

3. Sift the flour and baking powder into a large bowl and add the butter, sugar, eggs and vanilla extract. Beat well until the mixture is smooth, then stir in the orange rind and chopped orange.

4. Spoon the mixture into the prepared tin and smooth the surface with a palette knife. Sprinkle the chocolate chips over the top, spreading to the edges with a palette knife. Bake in the preheated oven for 35–40 minutes, or until risen, firm and golden brown.

5. For the sauce, place the chocolate, butter and orange juice in a saucepan and heat gently, stirring, until melted and smooth. Serve the cake warm, topped with the reserved orange segments and with the sauce spooned over the top.

Serves 6

oil or melted butter, for greasing

2 oranges

175 g/6 oz plain white flour

2 tsp baking powder

175 g/6 oz unsalted butter, softened

175 g/6 oz golden caster sugar

3 eggs, beaten

1 tsp vanilla extract

100 g/3½ oz plain chocolate chips

Sauce

85 g/3 oz plain chocolate, broken into pieces

40 g/1½ oz unsalted butter

3 tbsp orange juice

Prune & Armagnac Cake

1. Place the prunes in a pan with the apple juice and bring to the boil. Reduce the heat and simmer gently for 10 minutes, until the liquid is absorbed. Spoon over the armagnac and leave to cool completely.

2. Preheat the oven to 160°C/325°F/Gas Mark 4. Grease and line a 23-cm/9-inch round cake tin.

3. Sift the flour and baking powder into a large bowl and add the butter, muscovado sugar, eggs and vanilla extract. Beat well until the mixture is smooth.

4. Spoon the mixture into the prepared tin and smooth the surface with a palette knife. Drain the prunes well, reserving the juices, and arrange the prunes over the mixture in a single layer.

5. Bake in the preheated oven for 40–50 minutes, or until risen, firm and golden brown.

6. Turn out onto a warmed serving plate and spoon over the reserved juices. Sprinkle with the demerara sugar and serve in slices, with cream or yogurt.

Serves 8

300 g/10½ oz ready-to-eat pitted prunes

150 ml/5 fl oz apple juice

3 tbsp armagnac or port

* oil or melted butter, for greasing

* 175 g/6 oz plain white flour

2 tsp baking powder

* 175 g/6 oz unsalted butter, softened

* 175 g/6 oz light muscovado sugar

* 3 eggs, beaten

* 1 tsp vanilla extract

1 tbsp demerara sugar

cream or yogurt, to serve

Rich Walnut Squares

1. Preheat the oven to 160°C/325°F/Gas Mark 3. Grease and line a 23-cm/9-inch square cake tin.

2. Sift the flour and baking powder into a large bowl and add the butter, sugar, eggs and coffee extract. Beat well until the mixture is smooth, then stir in the crème fraîche and chopped walnuts.

3. Spoon the mixture into the prepared tin and smooth the surface with a palette knife. Bake in the preheated oven for 40–50 minutes, or until risen and firm to the touch.

4. Leave to cool in the tin for 2–3 minutes, then turn out and cut into squares. Place the crème fraîche and maple syrup in a small saucepan and heat gently, stirring until melted and smooth.

5. Top each square of cake with a walnut half, spoon over the warm sauce and serve immediately.

Makes 9

* oil or melted butter, for greasing
* 175 g/6 oz plain white flour
* 1 tbsp baking powder
* 175 g/6 oz unsalted butter, softened
* 175 g/6 oz light muscovado sugar
* 3 eggs, beaten
* 1 tsp coffee extract
* 2 tbsp crème fraîche
* 55 g/2 oz walnuts, finely chopped, plus extra walnut halves to decorate

Sauce
4 tbsp crème fraîche
3 tbsp maple syrup

97

Hot Espresso Cakes

1. Preheat the oven to 180°C/350°F/Gas Mark 4. Grease and line an 18 x 28-cm/7 x 11-inch rectangular cake tin.

2. Sift the flour, baking powder and cocoa into a large bowl and add the butter, sugar, eggs and vanilla extract. Beat well until the mixture is smooth, then beat in the coffee.

3. Spoon the mixture into the prepared tin and smooth the surface with a palette knife. Bake in the preheated oven for 30–35 minutes, or until risen, firm and golden brown.

4. Meanwhile, mix the cornflour with 2 tablespoons of the coffee, then add to a saucepan with the remaining coffee, the cream and sugar. Heat gently, stirring, until boiling, then reduce the heat and stir for 2 minutes, or until slightly thickened.

5. Using a 9-cm/3½-inch plain biscuit cutter, stamp out six rounds from the cake (trimmings can be eaten cold). Place on warmed serving plates and sprinkle each with a few sugar crystals. Spoon over the sauce and serve.

Makes 6

- oil or melted butter, for greasing
- 175 g/6 oz plain white flour
- 1 tbsp baking powder
- 1 tbsp cocoa powder
- 175 g/6 oz unsalted butter, softened
- 175 g/6 oz light muscovado sugar
- 3 eggs, beaten
- 1 tsp vanilla extract
- 3 tbsp strong espresso coffee, cooled
- brown sugar crystals, to serve

Sauce
- 1 tbsp cornflour
- 200 ml/7 fl oz strong espresso coffee
- 100 ml/3½ fl oz single cream
- 40 g/1½ oz light muscovado sugar

Warm White Chocolate Macadamia Ring

1. Preheat the oven to 180°C/350°F/Gas Mark 4. Grease a 1.5-litre/2¾-pint ring cake tin, preferably non-stick.

2. Place the chocolate, milk and vanilla extract in a small pan and heat gently, stirring occasionally, until just melted and smooth. Remove from the heat.

3. Sift the flour and baking powder into a large bowl and add the butter, sugar and eggs. Beat well until the mixture is smooth, then beat in the melted chocolate mixture. Stir in the macadamia nuts, mixing evenly.

4. Spoon the mixture into the prepared tin and smooth the surface with a palette knife. Bake in the preheated oven for 35–40 minutes, or until risen, firm and golden brown.

5. For the sauce, place the chocolate, cream and vanilla extract in a saucepan and heat gently until melted and smooth.

6. Leave the cake to cool in the tin for 2–3 minutes, then turn out carefully onto a warmed serving plate. Drizzle the sauce over the cake and sprinkle with macadamia nuts, then serve in thick slices.

Serves 8

- oil or melted butter, for greasing
- 70 g/2½ oz white chocolate, broken into pieces
- 2 tbsp milk
- 1 tsp vanilla extract
- 175 g/6 oz plain white flour
- 1 tbsp baking powder
- 175 g/6 oz unsalted butter, softened
- 175 g/6 oz caster sugar
- 3 eggs, beaten
- 55 g/2 oz macadamia nuts, finely chopped, plus extra to decorate

Sauce
- 100 g/3½ oz white chocolate, broken into pieces
- 125 ml/4 fl oz single cream
- ½ tsp vanilla extract

Currant Slices with Spiced Apple Syrup

1. Place the currants, cinnamon stick and apple juice in a saucepan and bring to the boil. Remove from the heat and leave to stand for several hours or overnight. Drain the currants thoroughly, pressing the juices through a sieve, reserving the juices and cinnamon stick. Set aside the currants.

2. Preheat the oven to 180°C/350°F/Gas Mark 4. Grease and line a 30 x 23-cm/12 x 9-inch rectangular cake tin.

3. Sift the flour and baking powder into a large bowl and add the butter, sugar, eggs and vanilla extract. Beat well until the mixture is smooth.

4. Stir half the reserved currants into the mixture and spoon into the prepared tin. Spread the remaining currants over the top. Bake in the preheated oven for 30–35 minutes, or until risen, firm and golden brown.

5. Meanwhile, boil the reserved juices and cinnamon stick rapidly to reduce by about half, until slightly syrupy. Discard the cinnamon stick.

6. Cut the cake into slices and serve warm with the hot syrup spooned over.

Makes 8

175 g/6 oz currants

1 cinnamon stick

300 ml/10 fl oz apple juice

* oil or melted butter, for greasing

* 175 g/6 oz plain white flour

2 tsp baking powder

* 175 g/6 oz unsalted butter, softened

* 175 g/6 oz caster sugar

* 3 eggs, beaten

* 1 tsp vanilla extract

100

Greek Yogurt & Honey Cake

1. Preheat the oven to 160°C/325°F/Gas Mark 3. Grease a 23-cm/9-inch round cake tin and line the base with baking paper.

2. Sift the flour and baking powder into a large bowl and add the yogurt, honey, sugar, eggs and vanilla extract. Beat well until the mixture is smooth.

3. Pour the mixture into the prepared tin. Bake in the preheated oven for 45–55 minutes, or until risen, firm and golden brown.

4. Leave to cool in the tin for 2–3 minutes, then turn out onto a serving plate. For the lemon sauce, place the honey, lemon juice and butter in a small saucepan and bring to the boil. Boil for a few minutes, stirring, until reduced and syrupy.

5. Serve the cake in slices with the lemon sauce poured over.

Serves 6–8

* oil or melted butter, for greasing
* 175 g/6 oz plain white flour
* 1 tbsp baking powder
* 175 g/6 oz Greek-style yogurt
* 100 g/3½ oz Greek honey
* 75 g/2½ oz light muscovado sugar
* 3 eggs, beaten
* 1 tsp vanilla extract

Lemon sauce
2 tbsp Greek honey
2 tbsp lemon juice
25 g/1 oz unsalted butter